ANXIETY IN RELATIONSHIP

Ultimate Guide how to Eliminate Anxiety in the Couple, Manage Negative Situations, Overcome Jealousy and Prevent Bad Thoughts

BY:

Lydia Sanders

TABLE OF CONTENTS

INTRODUCTION

Your first instinct is probably to conceal your relationship anxiety, especially if you know that your fears are overblown. After all, nobody wants to be emotional or overwhelming. Nevertheless, this is the tricky thing about anxiety: although it often feels only in a relationship by a single party, Ivankovich says that it is both the issue.

You will communicate as clearly as possible about what trouble you and why if you are an anxious partner. "Is it from previous baggage the anxiety?" She says. "The nervous person must be able to recognize the worries honestly. Don't you feel wanted, needed, valued, or like you're the one? Is there no emotionally intimate connection between the relationship? Is the relationship not physically intimate?" It's where I fell short as a friend. Anxiety can be difficult to put into words; it sounds noisy, frenzied, confused. When I was in a medical crisis earlier this year, I reduced the severity of the problem to my long-term friend. I was not entirely honest about my feelings at the same time, he seemed far away; I was concerned that he was pushing me away, when I was actually pulled away. Ivankovich suggests you can behave in ways that can exacerbate the problem and actually push your partner away when you have a stimulus to anxiety.

I tried to talk to my ex about my insecurity about my relationship, but in whispers, not overt questions. I didn't have any idea where to begin. If you are uncertain too, this is the formula: identify the source of the fear, tell your partner the source, and propose a solution. "If a partner knows the root of the fear, it's easier to deal with it," says Ivankovich. "In fact, there should be no problem without a solution. Tell them what you think you need to feel safer. Perhaps you need reassurance, perhaps you need them to be less confidential as to who they text. Give your partner an update on your feelings. "I finally made several (unnecessary, damaging) questions later and after. I said I often need more stability in my relationships if I am not consistent in one area of my life, as I have continuously fluctuating health symptoms. When I ruminate more than usual, if it doesn't text as regularly, or if it skips a telephone date or two, I begin to worry that he will go.

If you have no fear but your partner, you can definitely help with an acceptance and support attitude. Ivankovich says relationship anxiety is also your problem as the effects affect both partners. "Each partner must work to ensure that the other partner feels safe," says Ivankovich. It means listening attentively, asking questions, being always straightforward and talking more often than you might like.

CHAPTER 1:
OVERVIEW OF ANXIETY IN RELATIONSHIP

Each and every relationship is a little schizophrenic. Every relationship is somewhat schizophrenic. There is a natural tendency to be closer to the person you have some relation with. A desire to come closer by sharing your thoughts, pleasures, dreams and desires.

At the same time, there is a natural tendency to want to distance himself from him. The desire for independence, vulnerability avoidance, remains free and unburdened.

Both these inclinations are natural and create a healthy twilight and flow when they are finished mature, which helps relationships to mature gradually.

Both powers push and pull build a type of interpersonal dance. No, not a congo or macarana side.

This is more like the pairing of skating figures where one moment, hand in hand, man and woman are together and in the next instant are far apart, but linked by a shared rhythm. Although they remain connected at the opposite ends of the rink to music guided by the same choreographed routine.

But, what would happen if one of the figure skaters could not maintain the rhythm? What if one team member declined to meet the other? But did he refuse to be segregated from the other? They would suffer from their success. Badly. Badly. It may be called "Awkward On Ice."

Anxiety can easily spill into our relationships and create the same kind of problem. Some of us are plagued by the fear of being similar to others. These anxieties also centered on feelings of weakness, inadequacy or the fear of assuming responsibility. The solution to these feelings is very often to find ways to gain emotional distance.

These connections often do not gain momentum. They stumble, lose direction and ultimately die of a lack of deep connection.

A different kind of anxiety around relationships is the reverse. This insecurity will contribute to one's attachment to others. Your partner, friend or even your child's freedom can sound frightening.

Such fears often lead one to demand intense attention, affection and time from a partner. There is a reliance on constant reassurance. The person who receives these requests will easily be drained. Each attempt to show true love and commitment is never enough. It is never enough.

Such relationships break up under pressure.

Anxiety has crush-related capabilities. However, even if a relationship survives this stress, you can not depend on it to be as complete and fulfilling as anxiety would be out of the picture.

Bear in mind that the kind of anxiety we concentrate on has a specific connection with concerns of commitment and emotional intimacy. This differs from social anxiety, panic, phobia and other anxiety disorders.

Each of these worries can have a major impact on relations, but none of them are specifically concerned about emotional intimacy. The distinction differentiates how fear is surmounted.

SIGNS THAT ANXIETY IS FOR YOUR LIFE

You may wonder if relational anxiety causes trouble in your life. It can be hard to know. After all, everyone is nervous to some degree, so how you can tell if your relationships with family and friends have been affected.

The following questions can clarify if this is a problem:

1. Often do you worry that your partner will leave you for another person?

2. If he or she is out with friends, do you trust your partner?

3. Do you often require reassurance of the love and devotion of your partner?

4. Should you worry about how your partner is going to respond to a mistake you made?

5. Are there any talks that you avoid with your partner because you're worried he or she'll get angry?

6. Are you still afraid that your partner is unfaithful?

7. Are you someone who's getting jealous easily?

8. Do you have to control the time of your partner, know in detail where he or she was and with whom?

9. Do you not depend on your partner?

10. Would you feel uncomfortable if your partner depends on you emotionally?

11. Have a number of people said you're hard to get to know?

If you replied' yes' to five or more of the questions, it would be nice to have a very honest talk with your partner. Talk frankly about your anxieties. Try to understand how you can influence your relationship in trying to cope with these fears. Then, work as a team to see how changes can be made, how you connect and improve relationships.

In case you want a clearer sense of how anxiety affects your life, you can complete a three-minute' Brief Anxiety Quiz' on the next page.

What You Can Do To Combat Anxiety

To combat anxiety, it is useful to know the three main ways in which it appears in your life. Once you know how it appears, it is easier to figure out how to get it going.

There are three ways to show anxiety-emotions, attitudes and thoughts. The emotional aspect is what everyone talks about when they talk about anxiety. It is the concern and fear that will grow inside you when anxiety has begun to take root.

Physical signs such as increased heart rate, gastrointestinal discomfort, suddenness, fidgetiness, pacing, sleeplessness, etc.

The thoughts or cognitive effects depend on the anxiety target. Such reflections, however, usually focus on the catastrophic effects of certain events.

These three facets of anxiety coexist. Anxious thoughts produce disturbing feelings that cause you to behave in certain ways. For example, if there has been a severe storm and your spouse comes home from work two hours late, then you might start wondering if he or she is in an accident. That thought causes fear, which in turn leads you to start fast. The thought, the feeling and the action link each other.

We not only bind, we can also start to influence each other in ways that are not helpful. They are related to each other in a sequence.

An example should illustrate how this works. Picture Brian and Alicia, a young couple. We have been together for almost a year and are really happy.

Previously, Brian was concerned that his career was not progressing quickly enough. He wants to marry Alicia and wants to raise his income before proposing it. In this respect, Brian is determined to be a good supplier and feels unsure of his abilities.

This concern grew stronger later, and as a result Brian became more worried. The idea of "Loser" being graved across his brow is distracting. Yeah, Brian's really complicated with himself.

He wants to work longer hours to start his career (although he works 50 hours a week). As a timid man, a retired man, he doesn't tell Alicia. She will simply ask why and then he will have to tell her about his fears about "Loser" and it's very humiliating. Nope, he'll take care of this at the bottom in his own way.

Over the next few weeks Alicia frequently wonders why Brian is so distracted while together. She also starts feeling a little neglected, as he spends a lot of time at work. She says to herself "Weird."

Alicia has no background to grasp these changes without knowing why Brian is distracted or working additional hours. She assumes it must be because she no longer finds it attractive or interesting. Alicia begins thinking about the dedication of Brian to his relationship. She would like to talk to Brian about her concerns, but she won't risk being told her suspicions are right. It'd be catastrophic.

Then, Alicia wants to dial her own and withdraws emotionally.

Over time, Brian assumes Alicia's being less careful and affectionate is a sign that she needs more time for herself. He thinks "maybe I moved her too hard" and agrees he will respect her distance requirement. It can do this by working more in the office and not disturbing it by demanding too much of its time.

Naturally, Alicia believes that Brian's support in this way confirms his lack of interest (or self-absorption). Her fear and anger are becoming ever greater.

She starts to inquire if she is supposed to end the relationship before she gets hurt. We can see how this process is increasing and expanding with time.

HOW TO IDENTIFY AND GET RID OF RELATIONSHIP ANXIETY

I don't think any human being who is attracted to other people can say that they never felt concerned about a relationship, but relationship fear takes things to another degree.

It is the direct result of your relationship feeling insecure. You are worried about all sorts of things that might have a negative effect or ruin your relationship.

If you have had bad experiences in the past, your brain will have learned to respond in a way and expect trends to happen again.

You could live with constant rates of underlying anxiety about your relationship or it could cause waves of tiny, seemingly insignificant things. You doubt yourself and doubt the feelings of your partner towards you.

When you think what you are feeling might be anxiety about relationships, these telling signs will help you identify whether it really is a concern for you.

1. *You Believe the End is Near*

No matter how well your relationship is doing, you can not overcome the nagging feeling that you're going to go a little' Titanic' and hit an iceberg before you sink on board.

Even the least significant discrepancy between yourself and your partner has the fear that your odds have well and truly bite the dust.

2.   *You're Jealous*

Jealousy is a pretty common emotion, but if it gets out of hand no relationship can survive.

You will not necessarily show signs of jealousy that your partner will change their behaviour, and it may well push them away. But if one thing is certain, it will certainly make you miserable.

It's no wonder that you get jealous if you were deceived in the past, but it definitely makes you nervous.

3.   *You are Controlling*

You control your anxiety, which means that you desperately control your relationship so that you don't get hurt. You feel that if you have a handle on exactly what is happening then it will be all right.

4.   *You are too relaxed*

This may sound counter-intuitive, but one way to control things is to always go the extra distance to satisfy your partner and be the person you think they want you to be.

They can somewhat have no good reasons to bail out the relationship in this way. After all, every time they get what they want, so what's to talk about?

5. *You're reluctant to commit*

This is all about self-preservation. Although it may not seem so logical, you may be reluctant to lower your protective walls and move towards a more serious relation.

This may be because you are afraid that the relationship ends and that you do not want to be exposed to hurt.

Maybe you were burnt when in the past you committed yourself to someone, and this now fosters your anxieties.

6. *Questioning Your Compatibility*

You ask questions about your relationship with your marriage phobia, you try to find excuses why you and your partner simply are not compatible.

Often you find things so insignificant that they can easily be solved, but that's not how you see them. You see them as mines waiting to be seized.

(Truly, your anxiety may also be focused on real differences which may prove to be too broad to overcome convictions such as the way you believe about marriage or children, or where you would like to live in the long run.

7. *You get angry*

You're always on the brink, so it's easy to lose your patience if something happens that causes your agony. You do expect something to go wrong, so it's hard not to burst.

But, because you're insecure in your relationship, you probably worry that your explosion will change your feelings.

8. *You ask many questions*

You are never glad to accept an explanation. You ask questions and interpret the responses, bringing their words into your head and trying to find a hidden meaning.

9. *You do not enjoy sex*

This might be as a result of your uncertainty about the relationship makes relaxing in the bedroom difficult for you. If you are a woman, you fight to achieve sexual satisfaction as frequently (if at all), and if you are a man, you could fight to achieve it first.

Your sex drive may diminish because of these bedroom deceptions and your relationship's intimacy may suffer.

10. *Come Across as Cold*

Your relationship anxiety may mean that your partner thinks you're cold, stand-off or remote. You are defensive, and if they enter and then damage you, they don't like to expose any holes in your armor.

11. *You are too Clingy*

And, on the reverse side, your relationship anxiety may mean that you go completely the other way. You may need constant physical and verbal affections and assurances that you still love yourself and that you have not changed your mind since they were last saying it 5 minutes ago.

Overcoming Your Relationship Anxiety

Relationships is an awful thing to experience. This means you can't appreciate the magic of love, too worried that your partner will come out of it.

Ironically, your partner might want to put an end to all the negative energy that you worry about your relationship.

Luckily, you can do plenty to relax your mind and begin to change your outlook so that you can enjoy your relationship instead of living in a constant stress.

Here are some easy ways to overcome your relationship anxiety:

1. *Always remember that it's all going to be all right*

If you are in the middle of a disintegrating relationship it can easily feel like the end of the world. It can be extremely difficult to keep things in focus and see the light at the end of the tunnel when all those emotions rush.

It's as easy as to note that whatever happens, it's all alright. Think back. Think back. You have had heartbreak before, and you just got through it okay.

When you met your friend, you were perfectly fine, and life would go on after them if things ever go south.

Your life won't end if your relationship does, and being in a relationship isn't everything and not everything. A friendship can be fantastic, but it never determines you.

If somebody doesn't want to be with you, you can't do anything about it. You deserve to be with someone who moves heaven and earth.

When panic begins to rise, just murmur to yourself that all is all right. If you say it to yourself enough, you will start to believe it sooner or later.

However, the less you fear the end of the relationship, the more you can relax and enjoy it in the moment.

2.   *Discuss how you feel with your partner*

A lack of communication or miscommunications also causes anxiety about relationships, so it's best to talk with your partner proactively.

If you plan to see each other, be the one to look for concrete details, like when and where. And this does not mean that you always have to decide (though you want to share this responsibility), it does mean that you are the organizer in your relationship.

You could say that it's just an extension of being too controlled, but it's not. You don't drive any small thing by yourself, but you are talking about flying.

If your relationship is more established, but still anxious, talk from a place of honesty and openness to your partner.

Explain how you feel and remind them it's not they, but your past experiences. Try to provide examples of situations that are difficult for you and how they can alleviate your fears.

If the relationship is serious, you will want to do what you can to provide you with peace of mind.

It may also help you to express your feelings more pityingly if your anxieties cause you to do something that upsets them. You will know that what you say (or do) not necessarily mean all the time and that it can help you overcome your feelings by not adding fuel to the fire.

So asking your partner about your anxiety will actually make you feel better. In this regards, you will feel like a weight is lifted from your shoulders and you're confident that they don't go anywhere if they react positively and with love.

3.   *Build your independence*

If you're in love, you may feel that you're happy to live in your partner's pocket if you can, but losing yourself in your relationship is sure to boost your anxiety about your relationship.

If you just start defining yourself in terms of your relationship, you put too much pressure on it to be successful in the long term. Who would you be, after all, if you'd break up?

Make sure you do things consciously for yourself and keep a life apart from your partner. Try to retain the things that make you special, perhaps because your partner was first drawn to you.

Your companion is not your' other half,' and they are not finished you. You are fine and complete as you are. It's wonderful to be in relationship, but not important to your happiness.

4.   *Stop analyzing your every move consciously*

People comment throwaway. You don't ponder every word you say or evaluate how your nervous mind can view every text message you send. You should therefore not allow the little stuff to influence your state of mind.

5.   *Note that you control your mind, and it doesn't control you*

You're not at your mind's mercy. You have the power to guide, shape and train it. You may still experience fear once you've realized this, but you can recognize it for what it is and allow it, rather than allow it to consume you and guide your behaviour.

Breaking The Relationship Anxiety Pattern

Let's see how this kind of pattern can be changed in order to create more happy healthy relationships.

We will begin with a short one-issue question: the secret to getting rid of this form of disruptive anxiety is:

A. Take a psychoanalyst five days a week, lay on the couch, and say anything about what comes to your mind.

B. Burning incense, drumming, chanting, eating for six months a strictly vegan diet, and wearing paisley bell

C. A combination of clear communication and remedial experiences.

The response is, get ready......"C. "Clear communication was a gift, right? Definitely. Absolutely. Whether Brian or Alisha had been open about what they thought, the situation would very possibly never have spiraled down.

Then, it is worth noting that some people do not have clear communication sufficient to save the relationship. It occurs when one or both partners have particularly strong suspicions that they are intimate.

The anxiety is so deeply rooted that there is still uncertainty even with good communication. It's like talking to somebody who is afraid to fly and asking him or her about an outstanding aviation safety record.

The knowledge can be simple, precise and even scientifically acknowledged. But at gut level, he knows the plane on which he or she flies surely falls from the sky and crashes.

There is something else important to help this person conquer the fear of flying.

Corrective Experiences As The Key To Change

Corrective experience is essential to break the worried patterns we have discussed. A corrective experience is one that successfully repels any overwhelming fear. It rectifies a lie, it cures a distortion. To be corrective, the interpretation must contradict the very basis on which one's anxiety remains alive.

These bases are always based on falsehoods. "Nobody could genuinely love me, if they knew the true me." "I think people think I'm a success but that's only a façade- if they could see the facts, it would show me that I'm an impostor." "If I don't let that person work out in my life and things, I would be utterly devastated." Not by thought, but by practice. It's a dive into the moment that gives it energy.

Let me explain. Let me elaborate. Using the fear of the flight example again, a corrective experience would be a person who got on an airplane and remained calm during the flight (no screaming, no rolling on the island, no hanging on the stewardess like a teddy bear), and landed safely.

The person would have experienced flying in an plane safely and calmly. The lie "If I get on that plane, I will crash and die" has been falsified. Score one step for truth and get rid of the fear of flying.

However, to thoroughly reduce this concern, corrective experience would have to be repeated in various settings over a period of time. In this case the person would have to take other short and long flights with his companions and solo from different airports.

The hope is that the discomfort of several corrective encounters should be fully resolved so that it is no longer an active force in one's life. This is democracy. Democracy.

Success Story: Brian And Alicia Corrective Experiences

Encounters This young couple of corrective encounters would have required a lot of different behavior. With respect to Brian, it would mean talking to Alicia rather than covering her insecurities. It would also mean he did not try to work more hours simply to avoid his insufficiency (this means he had worked diligently throughout his career).

Alicia's therapeutic interactions will mean talking about her anxiety that Brian is no longer committed to the relationship, rather than avoiding talks. When her apprehension continued even after she was convinced, she would have to remain fully committed and attentive to the relationship. This is directly opposite to the reaction she had to avoid involvement.

When Alicia and Brian continued to act in ways that were counter to their fears, their fear would gradually decrease. With time, both of them could break the stranglehold of relation anxiety with repeated corrective experiences.

We would find a sense of liberation and emotional communication we had never experienced before.

Using this Information

The trick to using the story of Brian and Alicia is to make an honest evaluation of your own worries, anxiety and reactions to establishing close and intimate relations. Write down these and then consider how plausible each of these concerns is in your present relationship.

And at this point, it may be helpful to have a friend or advisor review the list and give your opinion on the relevance of these products.

Then pick those concerns that are obviously unfounded and seem to be major obstacles to the creation of a more fulfilling partnership. Take time to think about the corrective experience as a good first step to overcome this fear?

Panic that part not, just take your time. Take your time. Come up and be as specific as possible with several things you can do. Then pick one and go on to bring the experience into your life. Just as in the above example,

Brian had to talk to Alicia about his insecurity about his ability to provide. He would then have had to stop spending even more time at work.

This is the kind of realistic and "real world" insight to provide a solution. Don't get anything less to settle for. Initially, corrective experiences create anxiety. This is one of the reasons they're' corrective,' because you face something you're afraid of. If your behavior doesn't cause you to be nervous, it is possibly not very closely related to your anxieties.

In that case, you are unlikely to be very helpful. Do something that demands a degree of bravery. Then you'll know you're on the right path.

CHAPTER 2:
HOW TO DEAL WITH ANXIETY IN RELATIONSHIP

As we all that, one of the most pleasurable things on the planet can be relationships... but it can as well provide a breeding ground for anxiety, feeling and thoughts. Relationship anxiety can occur in almost any courtship stage. For many individuals, just thinking of being in a relationship will cause stress. If and when people start dating, they can have endless worries at the beginning: "Does he / she really like me? "Is this going to work out? "How grave is that? "Unfortunately, in later stages of a romantic union, these concerns are not eased. Yes, anxiety can get even more serious as things get closer between a couple. Thoughts flow like this: "Can this be the last? "Do I like him / her, really?"We ought to slow down? "Am I ready for such an engagement? "Does he / she / it lose interest?"

We can feel pretty lonely with all this thinking about our relationships. This can actually bring about a distance between you and your partner. At its worst, our anxiety can even lead us to give up entirely on love. Knowing more about the causes and effects of sex anxiety can help us identify the negatives that can undermine our lives of passion. How can we control our anxiety and be vulnerable to someone we love?

What Causes Anxiety In Relationships?

Simply put, falling in love challenges us in many ways that we don't expect. The more we love another, the more we lose. We are afraid of being hurt on many ways, both conscious and unconscious. To some extent, we all have a fear of intimacy. Interestingly, this anxiety always comes when we get exactly what we want, when we experience love as never before, or are handled unfamiliarly.

When we get into a relationship, we are not just nervous about the things happening between ourselves and our partner; they are the things we tell ourselves about what is happening. The "sensitive internal voice" is a term used to describe our mean coach who criticizes us, gives us bad advice and fuels our fear of intimacy. It says to us:

- "You are too ugly / fat / boring to hold an interest."
- "You're never going to meet anyone, so why even try?
- "You can't believe him. He is looking for someone way better."
- "She doesn't really love you. He's looking for someone better." Get out before you get hurt.

We turn against ourselves and the people near us through that critical inner voice. It can foster aggressive, negative and suspicious thinking, decreasing self-esteem and increasing unhealthy levels of suspicion, denial, envy and fear. In essence, it feeds us on a constant stream of thoughts which undermines our happiness and worries about our relationship instead of just enjoying it.

If we dwell on those concerned feelings, we are utterly diverted from real relationships with our partner. We can start to act in destructive ways, comment badly or become childish or parental towards others. Think of your partner staying at work late one night, for instance. Sitting alone at home, the inner critic begins to say,

"Where is she? Would you truly trust her? Perhaps she wants to be away from you. She tries to avoid you. She tries to avoid you. She does not love you anymore. "Such feelings will snowball in your mind, until you feel insecure, frustrated or suspicious when your partner comes home. You can be angry or cold, which then frustrates and protects your friend. You changed the dynamic between you too early. Instead of spending time together, you may waste a whole night feeling withdrawn and upset. You actually forced the gap you were initially afraid of. The fault behind this theory is not the situation itself. This vital inner voice influenced your thought, skewed your beliefs and guided you along a destructive path.

When all the issues that we worry about in relationships are involved, we are more resilient than we think. In truth, we can deal with the hurts and refusals that we fear so much. We can feel pain and gradually recover. The vital inner voice, however, tends to terrorize and disaster the truth. It can cause serious anxiety about non-existent dynamics and threats that aren't even tangible. Even when things happen, someone breaks with us or has an interest in someone else, our vital inner voice will tear us apart in ways that we do not deserve. This utterly distorts reality and destroys our own power and determination. This pessimistic roommate also offers bad advice. "You can not live. You cannot survive this. Always put your guard up and never be vulnerable to anybody else. "We have our own unique experience and adaptations in the protections we create and critical voices we hear. If we are nervous or unsecure, some of us tend to cling to our actions and be desperate. We may feel possessed or controlled in response to our partner. On the other side, some of us will easily feel intruded in our ties. We will withdraw from our friends and separate ourselves from our feelings of desire. We can act aloof, remote or guarded. These relationship patterns can come from our styles of early attachment. The pattern of attachment is formed in the childhood attachments and remains a working model for adult relationships. This affects how each and every one of us responds to our needs and how we fulfill them. Various attachment types can contribute to various levels of anxiety about relationships.

What Thoughts Perpetuate Anxiety In Relationships?

The specific critical inner-voices we have about ourselves, our partners and our relationships are made up of our early attitudes in our family and society as a whole. Sexual assumptions and attitudes towards oneself and others that our powerful caretakers had will invade our current perceptions. While the inner criticism of all is different, some of the common critical inner voices are:

Critical inner voices about relationship

- Relationships never work out
- People end up getting hurt

Voice about your partner

- Men are so unreliable, selfish and insensitive
- Women are so vulnerable, needy and indirect
- He doesn't care about you, he only cares about his friends
- You can't trust her
- What is so great about her anyway? Why so excited

- He cannot get anything right in his life

- He's probably cheating on you

Voices about yourself:

- It is not your fault if he gets upset

- You will never find someone who understands you.

- Don't get too stuck on it. Don't get too hooked on her

- He really doesn't care about you

- She is too perfect for you

- You can only get him interested

- You are better off without her

- She will reject you as soon as she gets to know you.

- You must be in control.

- Don't be too weak, or just get hurt.

How Does Anxiety In Relationship Affect Us?

When we shine light on our history, we quickly realize that our attachment pattern, psychological defenses and vital inner voices have had many early influences. All these factors contribute to our distress and can in many ways ruin our lives of happiness. Hearing our inner criticism and contributing to this discomfort will lead to the following measures:

- *Cling:* If we are concerned, our inclination may be to aggressively behave towards our partner. We may cease to feel like the independent, strong people we were when we became involved. As a result, we can easily break apart, act jealously or unsafe, or no longer participate in independent activities.

- *Control:* We can try to control or control our partner when we feel threatened. We can and cannot make rules just to ease our own feelings of insecurity or anxiety. This can alienate our partner and create anger.

- *Reject:* if we are worried about our relationship, we might turn to aloofness for one defense. We may get cold or refuse to protect ourselves or attack our partner. Subtle or transparent, these acts are almost always a sure way of forcing distance or generating uncertainty in our partner.

- *Withhold:* We often prefer to withhold from our partner, unlike overt denial, when we are nervous or afraid. Perhaps things got close and we feel stirred up, so we're going to escape. We have little love or completely give up on some part of our relationship. Withholding may look like a passive act, yet in a relationship it is one of the quietest killers of passion and attraction.

- ***Threaten:*** Our reaction to our distress is sometimes more violent, and we actually punish our partner. We can shout and shout, or give the cold shoulder to our partner. It is important to be careful how our actions respond to our partner and how they respond to our critical inner voice.

- ***Retreat:*** When we are scared in a relationship, we are able to give up genuine acts of love and intimacy and retreat into a "fantasy relationship." In this fantasy state we concentrate on shape over substance. We that stay in the connection to feel safe, but we give up the important parts of the connection. Often in a fantasy bond we engage in many of the above destructive behaviors as a means of distancing ourselves and defending ourselves from the anxiety that is of course free and loving.

How Can I Overcome Anxiety in Relationships?

To conquer the anxiety of relationships, we need to shift our focus inward. We have to see what's happening within us, independent of our partner or the relationship. What critical internal voices intensify our fears? What defenses do we have that can create distance? This self-discovery process can be a vital step in understanding the feelings which drive our actions and finally form our relationship. Through looking at our history, we will gain a better understanding of the origins of these emotions. What made us feel confused or turned on in relation to love? You can start the journey for yourself by learning more about fear of intimacy and how your vital inner voice can be recognized and addressed.

CHAPTER 3: HOW ANXIETY MAY AFFECT YOUR RELATIONSHIP

The generalized anxiety disorder (GAD) can have a negative effect on several aspects of your life, including your relationships.

These are two specific ways in which your distress can lead to problems maintaining relationships with others, and techniques can be implemented (under the guidance of a specialist in mental health) to help you manage there unhealthy attachments.

Being Totally Dependent

Many people with GAD hold their partners (or friends) closely and are continually relying on them for support and reassurance.

In addition to being overly dependent, people with GAD can feel inclined to overthink and prepare for all worse circumstances, be unable to reject and try constant communication (and be nervous if a partner or friend fails to respond quickly).1 People with GAD and overly dependent relationships can also be angry with the people they feel to be dependent on, ac.

Fighting Problem-based Dependency

When you develop overly dependent relationships, find ways to cope and rely more on yourself to feel better, your partner or friend can be put under pressure.

Of example, if you are angry or suspicious about these relationships, you should first note that this can be fuelled by your anxiety. However, take some time to think about any hard data (facts) which will help your interest in trying to gain insight.

A therapist specializing in a type of talk therapy called cognitive behavioral therapy can help you formulate strategies on how to reassure yourself and act on their own rather than needing the comfort of your partner whenever you are anxious.

Being Avoidant

Some people with GAD become avoidant of relationships as a means of dealing with their anxieties on the other hand. They can avoid negative emotions (e.g. deception or frustration), because they do not reveal their feelings, open them up or are vulnerable. Anyone avoiding close relationships may feel cold, emotionally unavailable, lack empathy or even stand-off, although they may wish for close contact.

Combating Avoidance

Cognitive behavioural therapy can be effective if you consider yourself too far from other types of therapy, such as psychodynamic psychotherapy. A mental health professional can help someone explore past and present connections and emotions.

Treating Your Anxiety and Relationship Problems

A therapist will also explore the impact of GAD on your relationships. Exploring the feelings more closely, for example, can be a good strategy for someone who tends to avoid relationships. On the reverse side, this strategy can backfire people who are more emotionally reactive and more reliant on others.

It is important to note that medication is often also a critical part of GAD care. While the anxiety medications, such as selective serotonin reuptake inhibitors or serotonin-norepinephrine reuptake inhibitors, are not curative, these can help you reduce symptoms and help you to feel better as you work with your treatment.

While anxiety can be healthy (it can motivate people and/or aid them to sense danger within their environment), it is overwhelming and debilitating for GAD people, which can be very harmful to relationships.

But be certain that you can develop healthy, long-term and fulfilling relationships with others with proper treatment.

CHAPTER 4:
WHAT TO KNOW AND DO WHEN DATING SOMEONE WITH ANXIETY

Being in a relationship with someone with problems of anxiety disorder can be terribly stressful. Sometimes it can sound like fear, someone who wobbles between you and your friend, is a third person in the relationship. This person always sows doubts and uncertainty.

Nobody has prepared you for it and you cannot choose for whom you fall. There is no high school dating class, much less meeting someone who is mentally ill.

Nonetheless, there is no need for anxiety to ruin the relationship or to make it difficult to enjoy. Actually, you can love each other more deeply by understanding fear in general and how it affects both your partner and your relationship. Education can also relieve a great deal of stress.

The book breaks down all you need to learn and do when someone is anxious to talk about: how to help your partner, how anxiety can impact your relationship, searching for your own mental health and more. Keep reading if you want to ensure that your partnership does not become a third person.

Anxiety-Filled Conversation

If you ask or deduce it after monthly meetings, there will be a point when your partner discloses that they have to deal with fear. It is a critical time in the relationship, therefore be sensitive and do not judge. Thank you for trusting you with this knowledge, which you probably did not share with many people. See it as the start of a conversation that you can often resurface.

Understanding Anxiety and Knowing What It is Doing to Your Partner

Learning fear and what your partner is doing will help you to understand and assist the partner with some basic facts about anxiety. Psychologist Dave Carbonell, PhD psychiatrist Dr. Helen Odessky, among others, suggested bearing these in mind:

- Anxiety is normal. Everybody's got it. It becomes a problem or disorder only if it is serious.

- Anxiety is a real problem, not a composite. It's a problem in mental health.

- Anxiety can be a crippling condition that prevents people from working and living a normal life.

- Anxiety causes people to experience flight and battle responses and worry about life-threatening issues, including whether a partner may cheat or leave.

- You can't "cure" or "fix." Anxiety

- Many people who have anxiety disorder wish they never had it. They are concerned that their anxiety is a burden for others.

- There are millions of people who have great relationships and are happy despite dealing with anxiety.

- Symptoms of anxiety, consistently or both, may occur in waves. People with anxiety disorders or problems can have time periods when they have no symptoms.

- Anxiety is not rational or logical. This causes people to worry about something, although there is no evidence that it is worth worrying. It also causes them to act irrationally sometimes. Your partner probably knows that.

- Anxiety is not a weakness.

- Anxiety can be treated. Psychotherapy can alleviate symptoms and teach people how to treat them better.

How Anxiety May Affect Your Relationship

When you are dealing with someone who is nervous, your partner probably spends a lot of time worrying and ruminating about everything that may go wrong or already go wrong. Listed below are some examples of thoughts and questions in the brain:

- What if he doesn't love me as much as I love him?
- What if he's hiding something from me?
- What if she is lying to me?
- What if he lies to me?
- What if he's going to cheat me?
- What if she likes someone else better?

- What if we break up?

- What if he ghosts on me?

- What if he doesn't reply my messages?

- What if anxiety ruins our relationship?

- What if I am only the first to reach out?

Most people have some of these worrying thoughts at least. They are a normal part of a relationship, particularly a new one.

However, people with anxiety problems or an anxiety disorder tend to have this anxiety more frequently and more intensely.

"Our thoughts are taking over and heading straight into the worst case scenario," said Michelene Wasil, a therapist who understands both personal and psychiatric anxiety.

Anxiety causes physiological effects, including shortness of breath, sleeplessness and anxiety. Anxious people can react to stress with the fight or flight response, as if stress were a physical attack.

Sometimes distressing thoughts motivate your partner to act in ways that stress and stress the relationship. For example, psychologist Jennifer B. Rhodes said, people with anxiety often check their partner's involvement with unsecure approaches. These strategies usually address one of their anxious convictions.

Let us say that your partner is anxious to be the first to initiate communication. You don't like him as much as he wants you to, he begins to worry because you do not send the first text as often as he does. Anxiety intensifies and he starts to think that if he did not reach out first, you could never talk with him.

He agrees that it's a good idea to fantasize on you a while to cure this fear. This forces you to communicate first. Perhaps a couple of times you'll touch him before he feels good knowing you'd make the effort. The proof encourages him to doubt his unreasonable and nervous conviction that you will not hit first. Though, it's clearly not a good approach.

Unfortunately, there are many behaviors in relationships motivated by anxiety. Here are a few more examples:

- Being controlling
- Perfectionism

- Passive aggressive behaviour or being avoidant
- Being overly critical
- Being irritable and angry
- Having difficulty focusing and being distracted

In case you are in a relationship with someone with social anxiety issue, the anxiety is likely to affect your social life, preventing or exhibiting offensive behaviour • Perfectionism Meeting somebody with social anxiety You may not be able to bring your partner to all the social events or meetings you want to attend. Like other types of anxiety, this may give rise to disagreements or cause you two to grow apart.

How To Deal With It

Anxiety doesn't have to jeopardize your relationship. You can have a healthy relationship through the right coping strategies and avoid anxiety from creating too much tension.

Encourage your friend to meet with a therapist. When you look after someone, you are tempted to support them by trying to act as a surgeon. The problem is that you are not a therapist. It will be emotionally draining to try to play that part. It could make your partner resent you.

You are not liable for your partner's counseling. That is why the partner should be carefully directed to meet with a therapist. A therapist can help them improve their treatment of anxiety in and out of a relationship.

If you have a serious, long-term relationship, seek therapy for couples. Some of the problems of anxiety can depend on your relationship.

Meeting with a couple counselor will relieve your partner from the strain. Instead of pushing them to do something for themselves, you encourage them to take part in counseling.

If your partner accepts or resists your suggestion to go to treatment, you should do it yourself. This helps you develop the skills needed to understand and deal with the anxiety of your partner. A therapist can also teach you how to support your anxious partner more effectively.

It's easy to forget to take care of yourself if you meet someone with anxiety. You can always reflect on your own mental health by going to therapy.

Learning How To Communicate Better About Anxiety

Anxiety can be frightening. You should make sure you don't think about it.

However, one of the most effective ways to deal with anxiety in a relationship is to talk to your partner openly, honestly and directly about it.

"It is crucial to have candid talks together about what they feel and to validate those feelings," says therapist Daryl Cioffi.

You need to encourage your partner to open up to show their anxiety. Try to listen, stand up for yourself, or take your fear personally.

Managing Your Reaction To Relationship Anxiety

It is easy to take it seriously and get angry when your partner talks about his or her fears in your relationship.

Anxiety can be easily understood as egoism, denial or a desire to separate itself, said therapist Michael Hilgers.

"You're going to want them to get over it," said Hilgers. "You'd like them not to think about it."

You can turn this ineffective default response into something more positive by practicing your coping skills. Here is an example to help you practice: assume your partner is afraid that she will betray you. When you take this seriously, maybe you think that she has this insecurity, because she hates you or because she thinks you're the kind who would cheat.

As soon as you do it, you can begin to feel frustrated. You might respond defensively and say something meaningful.

"You will only worsen the problem if you can't bend without bullying," said Hilgers.

Then you're going to strike again. Skip forward one hour later and you fight. The point is bubbling. Perhaps you don't even know why you fight.

Instead of making the tension rush up, take a moment to relax. Note that most likely the fear isn't about you. You're not the source. It's your partner. It's your partner.

Ask respectfully what your partner feels. Something like, "I'm so sorry you feel like this. That must be tough. Can we do anything to help you feel more confident about that?"

It's more important to manage your reactions than to manage your partner," said Talkspace therapist Marci Payne. It can help you be there and set boundaries for your partner. If the fear of your partner causes you to freak out every time you bring it up, it will not help you.

Setting Boundaries

You need to find a compromise between being compassionate and setting boundaries when you meet someone with anxiety. Once you realize how their anxiety affects their behavior, you can slow down them for behaviour, which you usually may not have patience.

Nonetheless, this should be minimal. Even serious mental disorders do not allow people to be cruel or hurtful.

"Not always be the bender," said Hilgers. "If you always give way to the fear of your partner, you will become resentful and angry, not to the anxiety, but to your partner."

You should tell your partner that these behaviors, including during anxiety and stressful periods that cause intense anxiety:

- Threats
- Insults
- Accusations

Endeavour to your partner that they are going to take steps to improve their anxiety. This is another part of setting limits.

Shifting Your Mental State to Relieve Stress

Anxiety brings about stress and we natural take this as an issue, nothing else. This is brings about fear and anger.

Dr Carol Kershaw, a clinical psychologist, recommended that couples try to change their mindsets on anxiety. We will grow a curiosity about it instead of just seeing it as a source of stress. Trying to understand the fear makes it harder to get angry.

"Curiosity will turn away anxiety and worry," said Kershaw. "You cannot experience two at once."

Supporting Your Partner With Relationship Anxiety Issue

The distinction between helping your spouse and becoming the unpaid non-official therapist of your partner. A therapist won't hold your partner while he cries or takes them out to alleviate anxiety.

The researcher Janet Ruth Heller, Ph.D., spent many years with her husband who has issues about anxiety. When his fear flashes, she reminds him calmly of what is going on. She also takes him to her walks, dinner or a film.

"These things make him feel safe and loved, which reduces his anxiety," she said. She said.

Her story shows that a caring and long-term relationship can be formed when someone is dating with care.

Below are some other ways you can help your partner:

Always acknowledge their progress on Anxiety Problems

Once your partner takes measures to work on fear, try to notice this. Alicia Raimundo, mental health advocate and speaker and anxious person, suggested partners "celebrate their strength" when possible.

Listen always!

Even if you're tired or feel like your partner is saying something, try to listen carefully. It allows them to learn that you care about it.

Do you have any rituals or hobbies you use to take care of your mental health? Do you have a partner? Perhaps you are meditating, exercising or hearing soothing music. If that is the case, consider including your friend.

"With boyfriends I have done breathing exercises and it's very personal," Nina Rubin, a life trainer, said. "We have sat across and breathed with the same slow pace."

Including your partner into rituals like these can help you both reduce your anxiety.

What Not to Do

In order to avoid aggravating the anxiety, creating more stress ad hurting your partner, do not:

- Dismiss their anxiety
- Criticize them for having this anxiety
- Allow maladaptive anxious habits by coddling them too much
- Take everything up yourself
- Try to be their therapist
- Try fixing your partner
- Recommend drugs for their anxiety issues
- Lose your temper or patience when it get worse

Anxiety can actually your relationship and serves as an opportunity to deepen your partner's understanding and love. The convictions behind their fear are part of who they are.

You can however support your partner by learning about anxiety or seeking help from a mental health professional to improve your own mental health. Your friendship can then become deeper and more joyful.

CHAPTER 5:
ANXIETY AND ROMANTIC RELATIONSHIPS

Sometimes it feels like a dangerous game to pursue a romance. Dating requires a degree of vulnerability and is likely to be hurt or frustrated. Thanks to the unpredictable outcome, people can be quite nervous about their current romantic relationship or the barriers to pursuing a new one.

Many find that untreated anxiety can affect their romantic lives. Individuals with a social anxiety disorder will constantly worry about how others are judging so they can avoid intimate interactions or dating in general because of their fear of embarrassment. Others with a common anxiety disorder may have issues with dating or maintaining relationships, because they tend to be worried about the loss of their partner. However, it is important to keep in mind that you do not need a diagnosed anxiety disorder to interfere with your romantic relationship. Everyone is vulnerable to daily stress, which is a matter of concern, fear of a partnership or difficulty interacting with a partner.

Anxiety Checklist

If you are not sure whether there is anxiety in your romantic relationship, consider moments or issues that worry you. If you are uncertain whether anxiety in your romantic life causes problems, ask yourself the following questions.

- Do you have that concerns that prevent you from entering into relationships or dating?
- Are you more anxious about sexual intimacy?
- Would you trust your partner deeply to comfort you or ease your anxious thoughts?
- Are you not talking to your partner seriously because you are afraid of conflict?
- Are you constantly afraid your partner will abandon you?
- Are you concerned while your partner is away?
- Would you allow your partner to be unfaithful without proof?

Steps To Manage Relationship Anxiety

- *Request help:* Never think you have to learn how to manage anxiety yourself in relationships. Consider how individual counseling can help you overcome relationship worries or take steps in order to make your life happier. Couple advice can also enable people to improve communication and develop problem solving skills in their relationship.

- *Create your own desires:* If you focus entirely on a romantic relationship, you are possibly nervous. Individuals with strong relationships with family and friends and focused attention on their own personal goals and interests are likely to become better partners and are less likely to experience separation or relationship uncertainty.

- *Assess your thinking:* Anxiety makes it difficult to assess objectively whether a concern is legitimate. Of example, if you are usually more nervous, you can be persuaded that your partner cheats or plans to leave you when no evidence exists. Discuss whether you need to work to control your anxiety by healthy habits, better connect with your partner or answer concerns about your relationship.

- ***Share the beliefs:*** People in relationships often concentrate so much on having someone like them that they fail to talk for their own interests and needs. Compromise is part of any relationship, but it doesn't mean that if something is important to you, you shouldn't express your thoughts or be solid. The sooner you can set the precedent for expressing your desires with one another, the less resentful you are.

- ***Don't run away:*** People who feel insecure in a relationship may be inclined to escape or remove themselves from problems that cause problems. Avoidance is just a temporary solution, and often ends in hot confrontation. Set a standard for resolving issues even if it feels at first uncomfortable. If you need a third party to promote better communication, do not hesitate to work with or individually with a counselor.

In case you're not really sure of where to start, think about your romantic relationship what you worry about the most. How can you deal with this issue in your best version? You may already have an idea how to improve the relationship and how to handle your own anxiety. Yet support is always available if you don't. Consider today who you can recruit to help you handle your anxiety.

SUCCESS STORY: HOW COPING MECHANISM CAN HELP YOU LOVE AGAIN

A mental health advocate shares her heartbreak story, hard work, and recovery Prior to diving into my life story with a mental illness, I want to tell you something first. If you read this, you probably also live with mental illness ebb and flow. In the rough days, desperate nights and unique challenges you may have a front line seat. And if you are like me, you might feel guilty that you always suffer, fight, or try to improve your mental health.

The next thing is for you. I share my story because I was there and I want to help. I want to help. My hope is that what I have learnt from my mental health–and the work I have done to get through it –can help you.

You must know you are worthy of love. You are also deserving of a kind and compassionate partner who loves you through the hardest days of your life. You are worthy of a love that embraces your struggles with compassion and gentle understanding. You don't have a responsibility because you have problems that go far beyond your control. I know that thoughts can be loud and pain can be intense, but you're still deserving at the start of each morning and the end of each night and in every moment between.

How It Started

The summer before my college year I started to experience hot flashes and sporadic bouts of swelling. I felt out of control at that point and was told that I had a heart attack or signs of severe physical illness. The more it happened, the more I became scared that it would happen again. I've always been in a nervous state of anticipation. I was reluctant to see a therapist and was diagnosed with a Generalized Anxiety Disorder (GAD) with my Mom's encouragement. Until that time, I had little knowledge of mental health and no idea what life was like for someone who lived with him. My "usual" revolved around university life. I concentrated entirely on the outside. Before that day at the end of the summer, I never reflected on myself; I never considered how I felt. My diagnosis marked the start of another realm of life for me. It was as if I was shaken awake— I think my entire mind was stuffed for many years.

Because of the extent of my symptoms, I could not return to school in the fall, initial summer, or subsequent term. My GAD developed into an agoraphobia panic disorder. Sadly, I was physically crippled and for months I couldn't leave my home alone.

It was a terrible time. I had a continuous state of fear and uncomfortable living, totally isolated from the outside world. It was surprising how quickly my life changed. Overnight, somehow, I turned from a wealthy college student — with a bright future— to a housewife in my own head. The agoraphobia was fueled by a concern that there should be another public panic attack. And, I wasn't ready to answer anyone I knew from the school and was bombarded with questions.

My new standard has been weekly counseling, constant visits and tests by doctors, regular mental health awareness and an obsession with bettering. Suddenly, my whole life was to save it.

In this difficult time, I kept dating my college husband. Depression, depression and heartbreak We had a regular and enjoyable friendship before my diagnosis–I thought of him as my best friend. However, my diagnosis took us both by surprise. Our unconcerned college romance suddenly went wrong with a real crisis in life.

We tried to do the long distance, but it was hard to adjust. One day, I walk happily through life together, the next day torn apart by a challenge which seemed at the time incomprehensible. He stared helplessly at me trying to fight for a life which had no pulse anymore. It felt as if I had lost everything— except him— I leaned even deeper into this passion. I kept on it like a safe haven in the storm's eye.

My worst fear came to light eight months after my recovery when our relationship ended. I can't talk for or about his acts, but I'm sure it wasn't easy or fun to deal with my situation. I experienced crushing pain that I didn't know was possible after our breakup. My mental health continued to fall, even faster than before. What was already heavier became heavier and my pain widened to depression and worsening anxiety. Losing him meant losing a former life's last sliver.

There was no escape.

Entering A New Relationship

It had been a year since I started dating Andrew. There have been no reference points or goals since I started working with someone new, but I felt confident that I would take that step forward after a year of focusing on myself. This time I knew that it wasn't going to be perfect, and sometimes I would have to remember who I used to be and who I was, but I did it — we did it.

In my recovery, I was far enough, but still in an active healing place. I had just come out at the other end of the most stressful season of my life and it was my main priority to preserve my mental health. As a proud promoter of mental health, I shamelessly told Andrew that I was healing. I filled it with all the delicate parts of my life and explained my daily work and self-care to take care of myself.

It had to be fully understood that my safety came first. These admissions came with fear, of course. After all, I wasn't an abandonment outsider. How could I not worry that my problems might be too much for someone else, even if I did have a year of finding out how to handle them?

Yet Andrew didn't bat an eye. A weight lifted off my shoulders— Finally, I got to understand what real acceptance feels like. It only had to be by the right person at the right time. Andrew's level of kindness and desire learning about my mental wellbeing and this made it so easy for me to let him in. However, we fell in love quickly and organically. Maybe, it was because I had a love to give that was designed from the ground up. However, it was due to the fact that he had a heart that saw me for me. Perhaps it was because life knocked me off my feet and I had the opportunity to begin all over again with a new sense of self and perspective. Perhaps it was all of the above.

Seeing the Struggle

I have taught Andrew how to be there for me over the years. The basic difference in this relationship is that I know my mental health now and I am qualified to advocate for myself when I am struggling. I discovered in counseling that it was all right to ask Andrew for what I wanted in difficult times and encourage him to be that for me. I learned that it was all right to be vulnerable. We have actually learned what has worked and what has not worked. We tried to find the right rhythm for ourselves. We worked hard to connect and discovered a language of love that satisfied our needs.

Only when we moved in with each other could he see the hard edges of mental illness up close. We spent the first four years of our relationship so we could not see all the dark corners of my mental illness. Call it timing, call it a milestone kick, call it work stress, but my mental health began to collapse after we went in together. I have been dealing with moderate obsessive-compulsive disorder OCD, my entire life, but it worsened beyond measure by the end of 2017. By May 2018, the OCD suffocated me to the point of collapsing. Andrew found himself unexpectedly sharing a table with the mental illness unforgiving, confusing and terrifying side.

I struggled with Moral Scrupulosity OCD, the constant concern that I was immoral, harsh, offensive, or uncomfortable. These obsessions may lead to repeated mental rituals / loops, finding constant reassurance and excuses. Sometimes I would find myself frozen, had to repeat a thought in my head until it "felt right." It consumed me totally and I once again struggled for my life in the way I had never before. Yet I thought about what I was doing instead of being quiet. I welcomed Andrew's help when he worked out how to give it. While it was out of his wheelhouse, he did his best to guide me through something that only my own verbal account could understand. And he asked questions, offered help, he listened, and he never stopped giving me the hope that I can go through it and maybe eventually get out of it. My life was saved by communication. Communication. Thinking about the pain saved my life. It saved my life to encourage anyone to be there for me.

Managing Mental Health and Love: A Brain That Is Loud But A Heart That Is Louder

While I was on holiday in Colorado, proposed to me in September 2018 in the middle of my recovery from my OCD. I can't believe it. I can't believe it. I had been battling my own mind every day until then (even moments before!), questioning my worth, succumbing to hours of emotional routines and struggling for my own life.

I had woken up early in the morning to do my OCD homework. I was on holiday, but he did not stop rehabilitation. How crazy it is to share the space on the same day with these two very different energies, love and challenge? I couldn't believe I got my most beautiful message in the thick of my struggles; I am still worthy of love. Although I have a brain that likes to persuade me, it was loud and clear in that moment; love always wins.

It was overwhelming for me at first. In addition to my current challenges, it triggered new anxieties instantly. It was totally new territory for me, after all. But I did the inner work to navigate it with any struggle I went through.

I sat with that anxiety, exhaled it into happiness, and after a few weeks I was able to feel disconnected. I have learned to turn to written or spoken words during periods of anxiety and fear. Whether I compose or I talk about my pain. Whether it's Andrew, the Instagram group (@anxiety support) or my own therapist, it always helps me to call for company to feel alone in my head. Writing was the most beautiful way I could do it.

Every day I'm doing my best, feeling my heart, working and knowing that I have a loud head, but a louder heart. I'm fortunate to have the best friend who never does the job for me, but with me. Next to me. Next to me. A partner who helps me to see fear not as a mountain which blocks the sun but as a mountain to climb. Here is love, here is mental health, here we are all worthy of both!

CHAPTER 6:
ANXIETY AND RELATIONSHIPS: HOW ANXIETY IS STEALING THE MAGIC

Intimate Relations are a mirrors that reflect the best and the worst of us all. They can inflame or soothe our hardships. They can feel like magic when they're right. Even if they are right, fear will steal the magic and loosen the bond between two people. Both relationships need trust, tenderness, patience and vulnerability. People with anxiety often have them by lorry and generously give them their relationship. The problem is that fear can sometimes erode them just as easily.

If you are someone who deals with insecurity, there are many things that make it easy to love you. Each relationship often struggles and when uncertainty is at stake, the struggles can be quite specific—quite natural and precise.

Anxiety can work curiously, and different relationships are influenced differently, so that not all of these are relevant to each relationship. Here are some ways to improve and secure the relationship against the effects of anxiety:

1.   *Upgrade the emotional resources*

You are probably super sensitive to the needs of others and give your relationship openly and abundantly. Sometimes, however, fear can drain these resources as quickly as you invest in the relationship. This is all right–there is plenty of stuff to do with, but it can mean that you have to make sure certain tools are updated. Heap attention, gratitude, affection, touch–a lot of touch–and conversation to your partner every time you can.

2.   *Let your partner always see you as a help*

Your partner may be reluctant to' burden' you with concerns, especially if those concerns do not seem as great as those with which you are confronted. People with anxiety have so much energy–without them, it is impossible to live with anxiety–just make sure that your partner knows how big or small their challenges are, sometime you can also support. Partners of anxious people may tend to dismiss their own worries, but this could mean they will not be able to feel nourished and encouraged by you–a huge loss for you both. Sometimes be careful to be the rock too. Tell, hold, touch, hold, and touch. Nothing cures more than the embrace of the person you love.

3.   *Let your partner talk about what you think*

While anxious thoughts are highly personal, encourage your partner to do so. It's a key element of intimacy. You also worry about what you have to do in order to feel safe, what feels bad for you and what might go wrong. You will also be able to think of other people–worried people–but be sure you encourage yourself to join in the thoughts that arrest you. Keeping things too much for yourself will increase the gap between two people.

4.   *It's okay to ask for reassurance–but not too much*

Anxiety has a way to get into it all. If left unchecked, you can doubt what is not worth doubting–like your relationship. To ask your partner for reassurance is totally all right and very natural. Too much, though, and neediness could be felt. Need is the enemy of desire and the flame will smother over time. Make sure that your partner loves you naturally, without being told–it's wonderful and even better for you.

5.   *Be vulnerable*

Anxiety can have different effects on relationships. In some cases, continuous reassurance may be required. In others, it can cause them to restrain themselves and reduce their vulnerability to heart disease. Vulnerability-open to others-is lovely and the essence of successful, healthy relationships. The problem with shielding yourself too much is that it can allow you to deny yourself. Part of intimacy is that you let someone in close proximity to the rest of the world. This person trusts in the fragile, messy, and untamed parts of you– parts often beautiful, often unbelievable, and always all right with the person who loves you. You can understand why someone should have open access to these parts of you, but see those fears for what you are– doubts, not truth–and trust that whatever happens if you open up to love and be loved, you will be perfect. Because you're going to be.

6. *Be careful to project fear into your relationship*

Nothing in particular will cause fear–that's one of the terrible things–and it will look for a target, an anchor to keep it still and make sense. If you are in a close relationship, the bulls-eye sits there and draws your fear to its gravitational pull. This can generate suspicions, envy, distrust and insecurity. Anxiety can be such a criminal. It doesn't mean your relationship is worth your concern–most definitely not–but your relationship is important, meaningful and often in your thoughts, making it a pretty easy target. Note that it doesn't mean that there is anything to think about just because you are concerned about. Worry, but then see what it is–fear, not reality. You're loved and you're anxious and you're all right. Let this be the truth you hold.

7. *Analysis ends in paralysis*

There is a saying that "thought leads to insanity," because it does. because it does. Is that love? And desire? Or am I myself kidding? What if my heart breaks into tiny jagged parts? What would it do if we didn't like the same music / books / food / films? What if we make reservations and the airline goes on strike? Even if we get sick? What if we get both sick? And if we cannot get a reimbursement? And pay the hypothecally? What if he makes me sick?Yeah. Yep. I know how it sounds, I know you know. How you concentrate on is what is important, so if you focus on the possible problems they consume the attention until they are large enough to cause their own problems. They can drain your strength, enjoyment and ability to move. You probably know this already, but what to do. Set a time period in which you can behave as if things are going to be fine. For instance, worry 10-3 every day and then relax, let go and act as if it was okay. You don't have to believe it –' act as if' only. Tomorrow you will have another chance to think if you need to. Be driven by the evidence, not the worries at 2 a.m.

8.　　*Come closer.*

When you focus on every aspect, things get wobbly. You that concentrate on things that don't suit your partner or relationship and seek confirmation that your partner is dedicated and loves you at the same time. This may cause you to put your partner off, then pull him or her nearer (Tell me you love me, don't you love me?'). Talk to your partner and, if it is a familiar process, establish a safe way for your partner to indicate when it happens. Agree on what's going to look like. When it happens, make sure that you do not perceive it as criticism–it does not–it is your partner who asks for consistency in the way you love one another.

9.   *Hard talks can bring you closer*

Both relationships now and then have to deal with tough things, but fear can make things more dangerous and more complex than they are. The tentation might be to avoid talking to your partner about difficult problems because of worries about what it could do with the relationship. Difficult problems don't walk away–once they hit a boiling point they fester. Trust that your partner–and you –will face a tough debate. Relations are based on trust, and it is important to trust that your relationship can be improved through difficult conversations.

10.   *Let your partner know what you are like*

We human beings are complex creatures and having someone closer to you and to your story–even if someone has been with you for quite some time–is the lifeblood of intimacy. People are changing, the stories are changing and it is even easy to lose contact with the person who sleeps next to night. Let your partner know what you're thinking about. Discuss how your feelings, anxiety, job, friendship, partner and love are influencing you, and how grateful you are for your support.

11.   *Let your partner know what set you on fire*

Is there a specific situation that lightens your anxiety? Crowds? Crowds? Strangers? Strangers? Entry difficulties? Loud in the car music? To be late? Talk to your partner so he or she knows what's happening to you if you find yourself in a situation without warning.

12.   *Be diligent. Be polite. The quick solution is not always the strongest*

As a means to feel better and ease your anxiety, you may be tempted to try to solve a problem or problem quickly. You may feel frustrated with the desire of your partner to wait for a course of action or resist talking about it again, while at the same time being open to your partner's viewing things differently and sometimes clearer. Breathing, communicating and not thinking the partner takes time or draws out of the discussion due to lack of commitment or because the question is inadequate.

13.   *Make sure you take care of yourself*

To be in love is crazy good, but it can take care of yourself and your special person away from you. We all tend to do that, but it can be particularly problematic for people with anxiety because once you've got out of control, the rip will bring other things up. It is so important to take good care of yourself. Well eat (a healthy diet rich in omega 3, low in processed carbohydrates and sugar), also regular exercise and meditation will help your brain develop fear. If you feel self-sufficient, think about it like this: it's not fair to expect that your partner will support you through anxiety if all you can do to support yourself is not done. Consider self-care as an investment in you, your relation and your family. Do note that anything good for fear is good for everyone, so talk together with your partner to pursue a healthy lifestyle–cooking, exercise and meditating... great!

14. Understand that your partner will need boundaries

The border that your partner builds can be great to maintain a close, healthy and connected relationship. Understand that boundaries are not the way of your partner to lock you out, but as a way to protect yourself from' catching up' your anxiety. Maybe you are stressed and need to speak over and over about it, but it doesn't necessarily make yourself, your partner or your relationship happier. Your spouse can love you and draw a strong emphasis from the last time you talk about something to the next time. Talking is good, but it can drain and cause a problem if you talk about the same thing over and over. You know that your partner loves you, and that it is necessary to nurture love and to develop relationships and not to oppose them. Talk to your partner what he or she needs to feel all right in the face of your anxiety. Giving the limits, helping to keep the relationship strong and caring and making your partner feel as if he or she can maintain a sense of himself without being overwhelmed by your concerns. Anxiety is infectious, so if your partner (eventually) wants to pull the barrier between your anxiety, let it happen-it will help maintain your relationship's emotional resources and will help you both.

15. *Smile together*

It's so important! Laughter is a natural antidote to anxiety's stress and tension. Laughing together will tighten your connection and when a stressful couple of days (weeks? months?) has taken place, it will help you both to recall why you have fallen in love. Anxiety has a way to make you forget that life has not always been taken seriously. If your partner has been seeing the type of your face when you laugh for too long, (which would be beautiful and probably one of the reasons he or she fell for you in the beginning), find a reason–a funny video, memories, YouTube... something.

To fall in love is supposed to be beautiful, but to get close to someone is not the best thing to do without being high and low. Intimacy is a conduit for any possible emotion from the happiness that someone pretty wondrous is as attracted by you as you are by them, to the pain of self-dodge and possible loss, to the comfort, riches and sometimes peace of a deeper love. Anxiety affects relationships but you can protect your relationship and make it solid, stronger and more robust, by being open to its effect and actively reacting to it.

CHAPTER 7:
RELATIONSHIP MISTAKES PEOPLE MAKE WHEN THEY HAVE ANXIETY

If you have an anxiety disorder, you know it could make life much stressful than it should be. This also affects how you feel at work, while you're out with friends, and even at night. Yet anxiety can also influence the relationship by adding tension, doubt, anxiety and the resulting mistakes and arguments.

It can be depressing to know what is worth worrying and what is not when you see the world through an anxiety-stricken lens. This can lead you to feel confused, to shut down your claims or to connect with your partner as passive aggressive. Although it is obviously not your fault, it is always helpful to remember how anxiety can affect the way you see things so that you can begin to move in a more healthy direction.

If it feels that anxiety really holds you back, you might even choose to treat it–for your sake and for your sake. "Seeing a psychologist is one of the best things you can do when you have anxiety in your relationship," says Katie Ziskind, married and family therapist. "If you are a therapist, you'll learn positive coping skills to deal constructively with your anxiety." And this can mean a healthier relationship by avoiding some anxiety-related errors, such as:

1. *Not Being Present With Your Partner (Being Absent)*

One of the worst side effects of anxiety is that it is "checked out" or not fully present in your everyday life. And while this sucks itself, it can have a negative effect on your relationship as well.

First of all, it can make "it hard for[your] partner to feel genuinely connected," says Bustle, a clinical psychologist, Dr. Paul DePompo. And so, because of these feelings of neglect, you two may have some arguments.

Nevertheless, it is an issue that can be overcome. If you are nervous, Dr. DePompo suggests you should make a conscious effort to be positive whenever you are together. You can also receive assistance from a loved one or a therapist who will show you how to cope with your fear and therefore feel more grounded.

2. *Having Trust Problems*

Because anxiety will make you feel like your life is being spin out of control, it is only because you won't necessarily feel safe. And this can lead to confidence problems in your relationship.

Rosalind Sedaca, a dating and relationship coach, tells Bustle: "An anxious partner can be more jealous (or) nervous than others to involve knowing who (their partners) are calling, texting and   (or) meeting throughout the day." "It can telephone or email (their partner) questioning (their) behavior too often and violating (their) privacy." Although it stems from anxiety, this behaviour can still affect the relationship and make your partner imagine things as follows. But this is only one more reason to seek ways of controlling anxieties and emotions, so that they are not overwhelming.

3. *Appearing As Controlling*

As people who are anxious to' control' their lives frequently cope with this, "Sedacca says. And it can start leaking into your relationship, which makes you feel controlled or manipulative towards your partner. While this clearly is not your goal, both of you can have a hard time dealing with it— especially if you have to go to treatment, learn safer ways of relieve yourself.

4. *Overthinking Every Single Thing*

Will you want to overthink everything? This is a huge sign of anxiety, and it can affect your trust in opening up to others— including your partner.

"The' impacts' of what you say can affect you," Dr. DePompo says. But if there is a person on the planet with whom you should be honest, it is your partner.

While some people can get used to it and some big faith, try to stop "editing," says Dr. DePompo. It may be daunting at first, but you're certainly worth it with a supportive partner.

5. *Taking Things Personal*

Then, another side effect of anxiety is that it becomes all too easy to spring to conclusions, take the worst, and therefore take things personally.

But it's crucial not to let your partner get out of control. "When[they are] distant, for example, a person with anxiety could take them personally instead of trying to have a conversation and figure out what could happen," Dr Helen Odessky, author of Stop Anxiety From Stopping You, tells Bustle, a clinical psychologist. "Examples include stress at work, physical illness and depression." It may be effective and train the brain–perhaps by using a therapist–to first consider these external causes before jumping to conclusions and picking up fights with your partner.

6. *To get "stuck" in old habits*

Relationships must be established and improved to stay healthy. Then, for someone with anxiety this can be incredibly difficult.

"People with fear stop trying new things, taking good chances and letting go," says Dr. DePompo. "This can keep the stuff standing overnight— you need a spark to kindle a fire. If you are, try things irrespective of how confident you like them — let them know about the experience and shake it about the perfectionism of' the best' choices."

7. *Always Expecting Your partner To Cure Your Anxiety*

While your partner should be aware of your anxiety and be as supportive as possible, it will not help putting pressure on them to cure it.

"We want them to ease our worries or continuously comfort them, but they are not to be occupied: specifically, to take over our anxiety," said Julie Williamson, behavioral therapist, LPC, NCC, RPT, to Bustle. "This is not just not fair to your friend, it is not fair to you because your partner can not cure your fear." You can deal with yourself by taking a lot of care, doing a few restful loves (like meditation or yoga), seeing a therapist or even taking medication.

8. *Replying Passive Aggressive*

As anxiety may lead to feelings of irritability, you may be hitting or responding to your partner in passive aggressive ways, says Williamson. You might also find that you can't talk to them without going downhill quickly.

9. *Venting to an Unhealthy Extent*

If you're not coping with your anxiety healthily, don't be surprised when you make the mistake of relieving your mate. While it's OK to let a bit of steam off and share some tense parts of your day, it can become a burden too often.

"If we feel anxious, we must be heard right away," says Bustle Melissa Kester, a marriage license and family therapist. "While we exchange a very noisy speech with all but the sink. Whilst we are monologuing in the expectation we'll be heard urgently, our partner can do us." There are so many other ways to loosen that your partner's ear doesn't always have. You could go to the gym, run, call a friend or leave everything with a therapist–everything will save your relationship.

10. Constantly Doubting the Relationship

When you constantly doubt the commitment of your partner or the safety of your partnership, it can help to step back and see if your suspicions are due to anxiety.

"People with anxiety have negative self-talks that can make them not trust that they are loved," tells Dr. Romancé's Guide to Finding Love Today Tina B. Tessina, PhD, psychotherapist and author. "This uncertainty will frustrate a partner and cause her to leave the relationship at last." To do whatever you can to reinvigorate everything is important not only for your own tranquility but also for your partner.

11. Getting Super-Angry

Like most anxious people, you can find that you are more irritable than you are. But if you're not careful, this might also snowball into anger.

"If you feel overwhelmed, trapped and unheard of, the nervous person's reality if you fight, can come frustration," says Kester. "When we share something important or try to stop feeling bad, our brain flips, our primitive self kicks in, we will blacks out, lose control of ourselves, and lose oral skills."

However, there are lots of healthier ways to get those thoughts out — or first of all to stop them. Then, therapy can be a great place to start, as can the above described changes in lifestyle.

12. Making Big Small Problems

If you have anxiety, you may have a breakdown over small things that would not usually bother you. As Sedacca says, "Anxious partners - lead to catastrophe situations, which cause things to blow up to be more or more dangerous than what they really are." This is another side effect of anxiety and can be handled through therapy. This is another side effect.

13. Avoiding conflict at all costs

One of the unproductive things in a partnership is to shut down. Yet that is what tends to happen when you battle anxiety.

"People who tend to be more nervous, tend to believe differences are evil," says Bustle's life coach, Elizabeth Su. "We often appreciate people and worry about the fact that if we disagree with our spouse, this implies that our relationship is doomed." Then, anxiety makes it difficult to see that arguments are good indeed. "What usually happens is an important conversation about something between you or both," Su says. Don't try to prevent your anxiety from engaging in productive conversations.

It would be great if you could snap your fingers and have no more anxiety, but it takes a lot of time to resolve it. But you can begin to feel better, and prevent these common relationship errors by seeing a therapist, taking care of yourself, or perhaps taking medication.

CHAPTER 8:
OVERCOMING JEALOUSY AND CONTROL IN RELATIONSHIPS

Ending jealousy is like altering every mental or behavioral response. It begins with consciousness. Awareness lets you see that the predicted stories are not real in your head. If you are so straightforward, you no longer respond to the possibilities your imagination might imagine. Jealousy and anger are emotional reactions that are not true to believing situations in your head. You should change what you think affects what your imagination projects and remove these harmful emotional reactions. Even if the reaction is warranted, envy and rage are not good ways to cope with the situation and to get what we want. Trying to change anxiety or indignation when you feel like trying to control a car skidding on ice. Your ability to deal with the situation is greatly improved if you can clear the risk before we get there. This means addressing the beliefs that cause jealousy rather than trying to control your emotions.

Dissolving relationships permanently means changing the underlying beliefs of fear and unconscious expectations of what the partner is doing.

The steps to end jealous reactions permanently are:

1.   Recover personal power so that you can control your emotions and stop reactive behaviour.

2.   Change your point of view so you can step back from your plot. This gives you a gap of time to avoid a jealous or angry reaction and to do something else.

3.   Identify the core convictions that trigger the emotional response.

4.   Be mindful that your convictions are not valid. This is distinct from scientifically "knowing" that the claims are not real.

5.   Gain power over your focus so that you can actively select your mind's story and emotions.

There are several factors that establish the envy dynamic. As such, effective solutions will tackle multiple elements of values, experiences, feelings and strength of personal will. You will leave the doors open to those negative emotions and behaviors if you lack one or more of these components.

You can step back from the story by practicing some simple exercises and refrain of the emotional reaction. You can do it if you really want to change your feelings and actions. It only takes the readiness to· acquire effective skills.

Principle triggers of jealousy are convictions which create insecurity feelings

Low self-esteem based on convictions of who we are. To eradicate fear and low self-esteem, we do not have to change our confidence in the false self-image. While some people believe this may be difficult, it's only difficult because most people haven't learned the skills needed to change their faith. When you practice your skills, it takes very little effort to change a belief. You just stop thinking about the story. It takes more effort than it does to believe something.

Self-Judgment May Intensify the Feeling Of Insecurity

It is not enough to "learn" the emotion intellectually. Only in this way will the Inner Judge abuse us with criticism of what we do. The Interior Judge could use this knowledge to push us into more vulnerability by an emotional downward spiral. You will need to develop skills in order to dissolve beliefs and falsified self-images and to control what your mind projects. The practices and skills of the audio sessions are available. The first and second sessions are free sessions and should give us an idea of how the mind works to create emotions. Sessions 1 and 2 also give you great exercises to regain some personal power and adjust your emotions.

One of the steps to changing behavior is to see how we create the emotion of wrath or jealousy from our own minds. This very step will not only allows us to take responsibility but also puts us in a position to change our emotions.

We don't take responsibility, if you're in a relationship with a jealous partner and want to change your behavior to avoid envy. Saying things like "When you wouldn't then I wouldn't react like this." This kind of language flags a powerless attitude and attempts to control your behavior by dealing with it.

How The Mind Produces The Emotions Of Anger And Jealousy

I described in the description below the mechanism of jealousy and anger. When you try to overcome envy, you probably already know the complexities I explain. This explanation can help to fill the holes in how the mind turns knowledge into self-judgment and increases low self-esteem and insecurity. This theoretical understanding will contribute to the development of consciousness to see these complexities when you do so. But you really need a different set of skills to make effective changes. You don't have enough details about how you build your emotional reactions. Just like realizing you have a flat tire, you didn't know how to patch the tire because you stumbled over the screw.

I will use a guy as a jealous companion for the example. I am talking about different pictures in the mind and you can refer to the chart below or see the Relationship Matrix for a more detailed description of these images.

It starts with a man who feels nervous. Insecurity stems from his "not perfect" False Hidden Image. The man creates self-rejection in his mind because he believes that this false image is he rather than a picture in his mind. The mental consequence of self-rejection is a feeling of indignity, vulnerability, apprehension and unhappiness.

Compensating for Fear

To overcome the emotion created as a result of hidden false image, he concentrates on his perceived positive qualities to counteract the emotion created by his secret image. The man creates a more optimistic False Image of himself from these attributes. I call this the Projected Picture because he needs to be seen like this. The mental consequence of a positive self-image is not self-rejection or indignity. There is greater acceptance, and he generates more love and happiness. Notice that he has not changed; depending on the moment, he only has a different image in his mind.

The hidden image belief causes unhappiness, while the projected image causes more pleasant emotions. It must be remembered that both pictures are fake. Both images are in the mind of the man and nobody really is him. He is the one who creates and reacts in his imagination to the images. In his imagination, he's not an image.

The mind of the man blends the projected image with the qualities attracted by women. The characteristics are often considered positive because women are attracted to them. When a man receives attention from a woman he links himself to the projected image instead of the image "Not Good Enough." The increased trust in the projected image leads to more social acceptance, love and happiness.

It is the recognition and loving behavior of man that changes his emotional state. The image or the attention of the woman does not change his emotion. These are only triggers which activate the mind of the man towards certain values, acceptance of himself and love.

The mind of the man also makes the idea "she makes him happy" or "needs" it to be glad. It only appears this way because he notices the relation between the woman and her emotional state. The man often does not know that his mind is only an emotional tool to express love. He may not have developed other opportunities to communicate his acceptance and love, so he relies on a woman for a catalyst. If the man realized that she is only a trigger, and that his role in expressing acceptance and love changed his emotional state, the man did not "need" his partner to be happy.

The contradictory False Images of the man may look in his mind like this.

Control Behavior

The man operates by the misconception that he is happier because of the attention and love of a woman. If he thinks that her attention is focused on someone or something else, he responds with terror. The main fear is not to lose the woman as he may believe falsely. The main fear is to stop the emotional pain that the secret picture produces in his head.

His Hidden Image convictions become true without her knowledge. His perception of himself also contributes to an understanding of this "not good enough" situation.

His feeling of indignity and unhappiness reflects his convictions and perspective.

The man tries to get and monitor the attention of the woman so that the trust in the projected image is active. He works to "activate" his "trigger" to support his belief in the projected image. It's the way that he uses to escape his Hidden Image beliefs. He does not know that love and acceptance are the keys to change his emotional state.

Punishment and Anger to Control Behavior

One of the mechanisms which we learn early in life is regulation of the attention and actions of others through anger. When we were disciplined as infants, this punishment was often followed by rage. Often harsh words were enough to make us change our behaviour. This got our attention at least when someone was upset with us. So we learned early in life to use wrath to control the attention of others and to punish the behavior of other people. We didn't necessarily unlearn this trend when we grew older.

The jealous man uses his partner's rage to get his attention and to control it. Anger sometimes serves as a justification for the woman's emotional pain. The woman can change her behavior by punishing the woman with anger to avoid emotional punishment in future.

The wrath of the man may not be his favorite choice. Yet his rage behavior is the product of a false paradigm of belief. The man can "think" differently in his mind, but his conduct rests upon false convictions and a distorted picture that drives his emotions.

The Actual Outcome Of Controlling Anger

The man gets the opposite results of his anger as a child. An adult has more power than a child to resist the punishment of anger. The woman will withdraw due to her tendency to avoid the emotionally disagreeable. Her retirement will then trigger her confidence in the distorted picture he tried to prevent. The creed-emotion process of the man comes back to the beginning. This is painful emotionally.

Analysis After the Incident

The study after the incident, There is an opportunity to look at and evaluate incidents after a jalousy and rage incident. This period can be emotionally more difficult for the jealous man. His self-assurance can be the worst of all.

The man plays the action of rage and power in his mind. However, it is now examined from the point of view of the Inner Judge. The Interior Judge analyzes the matter and condemns him. The inner judge holds the projected image specifically and then points out that he has failed to fulfill this standard. He can only assume that he's a loser and not good enough based on the predicted picture level.

The rage case, seen by the Inner Judge, is "proof" that he is the person in fact that fits the description of the Hidden Picture. Accepting this judgment and believing it, the man feels unworthy, guilty and disgraceful. The belief, feeling and perception of the character of the secret image are enhanced by the Inner Judge. It's a suspended lawyer. The judge does not evaluate the role of the belief system, false images or the viewpoint. The man is at the hands of powers, which he was not educated to see and deal with. He can begin to control his emotional state with awareness of these forces and certain specific practices.

Attempts to change behavior do not seem to work

The main problem in the study is that man approaches the events from a judgmental point of view. Judgment leads to denial. It also serves to improve confidence in the standard of perfection. This view strengthens the Hidden Image and the belief that the projected image is a core cause. The very thing in our mind that the research is doing is simply enhancing the core causes.

A man looks for a solution and the solution seems to become the' Projected Image' in this paradigm of indignity. But then, if he can become the confident, strong, kind and loving person he knows he is, then he will love him, the woman will love him, and everything will be fine. He doesn't see that his imagination forms the projected image.

This strategy has other issues

1. The man's conviction that he is the Projected Image is being undermined by his conviction that he is not "strong enough." Being perfect may sometimes compensate, but the sense of unworthiness passes until the hidden image is addressed.

2. Even if the man turns out to be the perfect projected image, the hidden faith in the image will feel like fraud. He's not really "good" and he's not "worthy," according to Hidden picture beliefs. He'll be unauthentic because of these conflicting beliefs. The sensation of being a cheat also arises when others applaud his achievements. The more successful and recognizable he is, the more prominent is the hidden image in his mind. It can't be emotionally integrated as long as he combines his identity with one or more conflicting images in his mind.

3. The efforts of the man to control his emotion will protect him from eruption of jealousy and anger. This "on watch" feeling emerges

out of the fear that emotion will consume his attention at any time. Not only does that feeling of fear affect a person, it also represses emotions and does not allow true love and joy to be felt.

4.   Strong positive values and a positive self-image can, but to a certain degree, help to reduce the reaction side. It is a patch that can support but still find identity in a false picture, not in honesty and dignity. He does nothing to resolve the feelings that are at the center of the actions from the distorted thoughts or the convictions of unworthiness. These are often hidden in the subconscious and then come back during times of stress when they are most harmful.

False Beliefs and Emotion Drive the Behavior

When one looks at the conduct of jealousy and anger as a means of controlling and holding others, the action makes no sense. Wrath and envy won't make anyone closer to us. The man can often look at his behavior in the situation and see that it makes no sense. As a result of his actions, he can see the woman leaving him. Seeing the outcome and knowing it intellectually, however, does not change its behavioral dynamic. Why? Why?

His conduct is not motivated by thought, reasoning or analytical understanding. It can not therefore be modified by these modalities. It is guided by beliefs, false images, opinions, and emotions. If we are to change our behavior, these basic elements must be discussed in a way other than pure intelligence and logic. Why do you use a different approach to intellect and logic? Intellect and reasoning will be used by the Interior Judge to make decisions and improve the current false beliefs.

Going By the Results

Changing attitudes, emotional reactions and destructive behavior is by overcoming the false beliefs of your mind, your focus and your point of view. When you learn to change your perspective, you can literally move away from confidence and emotion. From a new perspective, you are aware of the wrong logic of the beliefs behind your behaviour. You will be in a position to refrain from destructive behaviour, recognizing the false beliefs behind your actions. Eliminating the misconceptions eliminates the emotional triggers. It is the elimination of false convictions which will remove fear.

If you want to change a jealous and angry behaviour, you will have to do more than study the issue. You're going to have to move. I propose to continue with the free audio sessions. Practice the exercises for a couple of days and hear what you know. You will register free of charge. No credit card details are needed.

HEALTHY WAYS TO DEAL WITH JEALOUSY IN A RELATIONSHIP

Jealousy is not totally a bad thing, it's human nature. From time to time, it is natural to feel jealous.

Envy is troublesome "when we behave or wallow out in envy," says Christina Hibbert, PsyD, Flagstaff, clinical psychologist, Ariz.

It becomes complicated when he starts to overwhelm you and "creates into every part of your life," said Kathy

Morelli, LPC, a psychotherapist with a specialty of marriage and family therapy in Wayne, N.J.

Romantic jealousy is one of the most common forms of jealousy, she said. They are also jealous of the successes, talents, lifestyles and relationships of others, Hibbert said.

For example, we may think that the life of someone is much easier or more comfortable than ours. "We only see good and only evil in our life." Or maybe we assume that our best friend has a better relationship with another friend.

Social networking sites–like Facebook–can also cause envy. Today, our online and offline worlds overlap, and relationships and similarities are much more complicated and nuanced, "said Morelli.

Insecurity is often the basis of jealousy. "We're feeling threatened, or less or insufficiently healthy," said Hibbert. W]y fear that the abilities of somebody else mean something bad about us." (Jealously, too, may be a product of your previous experiences, but more later.) Below, there will be general tips for coping with envy, together with concrete jealousy suggestions in romantic relations.

Romantic Relationship Tips

- *Evaluate your relationship*

"The best way to overcome insecurity is to look at your romantic relationship first," said Morelli. Consider, for example, if your relationship is based on honesty, respect and love and if the actions of your partner represents their expressions.

Were they honest with you, were they honest? If you are not, this can actually cause or sustain your insecurities, said Morelli, who also writes the books BirthTouch ® for pregnant and postpartum couples, Perinatal Childbirth Professional Mental Illness and Healing for NICU Parents.

"When you are in an unstable relationship, expect your jealousy buttons to be pressed. But no one can say what to do to you. You may feel bad and jealous sometimes if you stay. "Assess yourself.

- ***Evaluate Yourself***

If you have a safe and strong relationship and still feel jealous, look at yourself and explore your own experiences.

"Research in a romantic relationship on the topic of envy indicates that a person's fundamental style of attachment underlie their susceptibility to jealous reactions," Morelli said.

Individual who in their early years have developed stable relationships–between themselves and their careers–appear to be less protective and dependent, have greater autonomy and have less feelings of insufficiency than children in unstable attachment styles.

Morelli asked himself the following questions: "Do you have an intense sense of emptiness or lack of self-esteem?

- Were your early caregivers not reliable?
- Were you raised in a repressive environment?
- How was your relationship with your early caregivers?

- Do you feel a lack of self-worth or pervasive feeling?

- Was the environment you were raise warm and loving and also critical?

The type of attachment is malleable, she said. Subsequent interactions and conditions will affect your style. For example, a professional therapist can help you develop self-esteem and deal with your issues.

Seek other support

Morelli said, have interests beyond your partnership. Discuss with a friend about your jealous sensations, "but don't do this to the exclusion of talking with your partner."

General Tips

- *Always recognize your jealousy*

"It loses its control when we call envy, because we're no longer letting it intimidate us," said Hibbert. Recognizing you're jealous, she said, opens the door to understanding.

- ***Learn from your jealousy***

Hibbert, author of the book ***This is How We Grow***, said we can use feelings of envy as a motivation to grow. You know, for example, that every time your friend plays his guitar you get jealous because you want to do it too. Instead of wallowing in that envy, she said, you sign up for guitar lessons.

- ***Let it go***

Tell yourself that in your life you don't need that feeling, so you give it up, said Hibbert. Then "respire deeply and imagine it flowing like the wind through you. Repeat as often as you need to really quit it. "Healthily control your feelings.

- ***Manage your emotions***

"Practice consciousness to soothe the weakening feelings," said Morelli. For starters, she recommended that readers tap into your body to see how you feel, take some deep breaths and try to separate yourself from the strength of these emotions.

She said, if your envy concerns your romantic relationship, once you calm down, share your feelings with your partner.

She also suggested journaling, dancing and listening to your favorite music to channel your feelings.

- ***Remind yourself of your positive features***

"She's very good at playing with her kids and I'm not so sweet. Hibbert gave this example. But I'm great to read to them and they love me. "She said that teaches everyone that everybody has strengths and weaknesses.

Jealousy is once again a normal reaction. When it becomes chronic, it becomes troublesome. Recognize what happens when you feel jealous and deepen your relationships and yourself.

CHAPTER 9:
NEGATIVE THINKING IN RELATIONSHIPS

Negative thinking patterns make life less satisfactory when they keep you stuck in what's wrong versus what's right. Negative thinking often interferes with what you really want. It makes you feel sad, depressed and unhappy.

If the glass is half empty, it is almost difficult in each encounter to see the positive, potential or silver linings and life lessons. In a partnership, it is extremely difficult for you or your partner to be content with this mindset. If your partner feels he or she can't please you and maximize your satisfaction, for example, he or she can feel less, weak, inadequate, etc. If you believe that your partner never does anything good enough, there may be relationships of friction, stress and frustration. This dynamic, unfortunately, can easily become a vicious cycle of negativity.

You earn the energy you bring into the universe, so that when you dwell on the negative you can see and get into your relationships. While unintentionally or consciously you may have developed false beliefs to shield yourself from damage or disappointment, it is time to create a positive change in order to maintain a healthy loving relationship. I understand that it may feel easier not to get your hopes on a new relationship (especially if you were previously heartbroke) but is it not one of your priorities to find someone who is amazing and thriving as a couple? If you have answered yes, this is an opportunity to turn your pessimistic lens into a more rational and positive attitude.

How To Suppress Negative Thinking

This is how:

1. ***Assess your beliefs about yourself, relationship, world, and what you wish for in life honestly.*** Do you believe like "Nothing works for me," "Men (or women) always hurt me" or "The world is a hideous place?"If your words sound like some of the ones above, you think bad.

2.   ***Take control of your negative ideas.*** Let us use the instance, "Nothing works for me" that feels heavy, definitive and permanent. Adjust this idea internally to create room to figure out stuff for you and to appreciate all that has done well for you. Talk about your memories and note that life has gone well for you many times. Try various positive thoughts and see what feels right. For example, "I am open to meaningful interaction in my life and love." "I am thankful for   "or "I can manage my life."

3.   ***Rewire your brain.*** Recognize and transform a negative thought or beliefs into one of the most positive thoughts you have developed. This is an unbelievably important change in your mind, so it takes time, energy and persistence to get the idea you want in a safer, new way. However, once you constantly correct it, you will see that your negative thoughts dissipate and healthier ones arise. This is how you take

down the negative lens and look at the world more honestly and with more hope.

A few other tips to make your dating and relationship life more satisfying as you change your mind in order to achieve the love you wish for...

- ***Always remember that taking care of your expectations are important to your relationship's success.*** Discrepancies and conflicts are inevitable in the world of relations, so remember that it's natural and all right. The most important thing is how you and your partner manage and develop in difficult times.

- ***Remember your partner is also a person.*** Not all your partner does is "right" or "good," but you resist the urge to change your critical lens when you are frustrated. Communicate on your desires and don't try to generalize the entire relationship for a moment when you feel hurt.

- ***Consider the partner deliberately in a positive light.*** Thank you for the little things and compassion that your partner shows. Say thank you. Say thank you. It perpetuates a cycle of optimistic and caring relationships.

- ***Don't take things personally.*** There will be poor dates, difficult conversations and times that can be frustrating at the time. Do not add these experiences to your negative pile–take life lessons instead and imagine yourself moving towards your goals. Engage yourself to be happy on your journey to marriage.

HOW TO PREVENT TOXIC THOUGHTS FROM AFFECTING YOUR RELATIONSHIP

There are all kinds of things that can ruin an entirely good relationship. Cheating and incompatibility, for example, are two major issues. According to experts, there is one thing that can more than anything else ruin a relationship.

The biggest killer of the relationship can be negative thoughts, "says Bustle, licensed psychologist Nicole Issa, Psy. D. "There is a very close feedback link between the emotions, feelings, and actions. Having negative thoughts will take you down the rabbit hole." It is important to know from Dr. Issa that your thinking habits will contribute to important problems with your relationships. For example, early childhood encounters with your parents can make you feel unworthy of love. That is why you may get into all relationships believing that at some stage your partner is about to abandon you, and you may be afraid to speak up.

"The truth is that we are making our own reality," Joann Cohen, matchmaker and dating coach, says to Bustle. "If we believe we have a good relationship, we work through things that believe that things are always ok. But when you come to relationships with negative thought, you expect always the worst not only for your partner, but also for the outcome of your relationship." It is important for you to find ways to make them positive in order to prevent negative thoughts. Listed below are some things you can do to stop toxic ideas, according to experts, sabotaging your relationship.

1. *Think about the first time you have fell in love with your Spouse*

When you pass a rough patch, it is easy to let that cloud judge you. Talk about the "real" feelings of your partner when you start invading your mind, the first time you fell in love with them, and talk about how you felt. "Shutting your eyes and seeing the bright eye person with whom you fell in love will make things look much more positive and doable," says Cohen. At times, we need only a little reminder of the good times to resolve the poor.

2. *Letting Go of the Past*

To be honest, letting go of the past is absolutely easier said than done. To be fair "We all have a piece of our history with us to' shield' us against getting hurt again," says Cohen. "And if you continue to bring your old relations and harm to your new relationship, then you sabotage and create the truth that things just do not or will not work." Then, try to separate your past from your present, to prevent your past from creating toxic thoughts. No matter how much they look, speak, or behave the same, your ex isn't your current partner. If you can separate your previous relationship from your new one, being more involved is much easier for you.

3. *Find other ways to channel your energy*

Toxic thinking will cause you to do unreasonable, relationship-sabotage stuff like hack into your partner's phone or sabotage. To counter this phenomenon, Dr. Issa says that he knows what your thoughts are doing. For instance, why do you feel you need to just "check in" your partner 20 times in a row? You would also want some affirmation or confirmation that your partner really cares. "Once you know that you have an ability to do (these) stuff, take some time to practice those skills to help you like to count to ten and relax," she says. Find ways to reduce the intense feelings you have so that you will not act in ways that you will regret later.

4. *Do not Assume you Know What Your Partner Is Thinking*

Negative thoughts are more often than not based on perceptions that do not always exist. "If we put our negative feelings on somebody else or place them on your significant other person, the anger of the other person is what you are reading," Cohen says. The important thing here is never to presume. Do not jump to conclusions. Jump to conclusions. Don't cook it yourself if you can't help it. Get to the edge and chat to your friend. "Try or ask for clarification, take the words on face value," she says. "You never believe you know how they feel."

5. *Have That One Person You go-to to Vent Your anger*

If you are mad about your partner, it's not uncommon to put all your problems to anyone who's listening. If you are mad about your partner. But, according to Cohen, "When you do that, you create a gap between your meaningful other person and your world, creating more negativity than you know." If you have to really lower yourself down, choose one person and stay with them. "Saying to everyone is not helpful to your ugly business and will only encourage more negative feelings," she says.

6. *Create A List Of Your Toxic Thoughts And Come Up With Positive Ones*

Preventing toxic thoughts from destruction takes some self-reflection with constructive alternatives. One of the best things to do while reflecting is to physically write out all the typical ideas that lead to struggles or even divisions. Take it a step further and write hard proof for or against any thought. After that, come up with a more concise and adaptive alternative thinking. For instance, if you think your partner is no longer interested in you because they didn't reply to your text, please list all other things they could do. "Think about other occasions they have taken a while to answer or to show that they're still involved," says Dr Issa. "Here the alternative thought may be as simple as' just as I haven't heard of them yet it doesn't mean they don't care.'" Then, the more detailed you are, the more effective it will be.

7. *Take Breaking-up Totally Off The Table*

Whatever the toxic thoughts are, usually they are from the same location — fear. In particular, the fear that your partner will leave. "I use the analogy, you' burn the ship' when you comment," Cohen says. "There is no way to get out of the island when you burn the ship, so work together to survive." If there is no solution, you start seeing what is good in a situation. When you take the chance to break the equation (that is "burning the ship"), you can support your relationship from a place of love and not fear. If your words and actions come from a place of affection, it's much easier for you to remain positive.

A thinking is only a thought at the end of the day. It's not necessarily the truth. If you don't let your relationship consume you, it will improve your relationship.

CHAPTER 10:
HOW TO STOP OVERTHINKING
IN A RELATIONSHIP

I believe that we are all over-thinkers, regardless of whether or not we are conscious, that is another problem. I used to overthink everything. It was like a good feeling that I had to have to work and especially in my relationship. How can I quit in a relationship?

I figured that I couldn't get rid of such an unpleasant and destructive habit. However, like everything else, practice makes it perfect, if you training your mind with the right commitment, you don't have to overthink your life.

Writing this article also recalled many bitter memories of the way I used to be.

I overanalyzed every little detail of what a friend said and how when we were together he expressed his feelings. It was so sick that I realized that this addiction would consume my life, if I didn't do anything about it, and I was the only one to blame.

Why Is Overthinking An Addiction?

A book by Dr. Sian Beilock Choke: What the secrets of the brain reveal when you have to explain this amazingly tiring event by quoting golf studies. They're a perfect analogy, as shocking as it is.

She says, when a professional golfer begins to think in the area, he is just a shy thought of missing the hole and losing the game. It's because our subconscious often paralyzes our body and paralyzes it anxiously just a second or two. The fear of failure is typically the one to blame.

Overthinking is persistent paralysis of a golfer. As many empirical studies have shown, when we start losing control, it is a strategy that we use. Errors frighten us, confusion is overwhelming, and much can go wrong. So, we always think about it.

My sister cried clearly at a golf court, I remembered because she could not play as well as I did. I wasn't a better player, don't get me wrong, but what helped me win the games came about because I didn't care about it, because I didn't overthink everything. I've been there for fun.

Addictive Behaviors

When you think about it, overthinking is no different from OCD. They ought to make life less unpredictable and give us a sense of control and trust. Only, we superintend our thoughts instead of establishing dominance over things.

In psychology, every conduct that is brought to bear by a necessity, the behavior that thus turns to the most important thing in your life, but that leads to a conflict between short-term activity and long-term impacts–is defined as addictive.

It is often obsessed with overthinking when we have to control our lives. The problem is that what starts as a tactic that should calm us down us usually leads us to lose control of our emotions. The vicious circle continues, with us in the middle.

Overthinking - Number One Relationship Killer

Two of my relationships ended badly because I'm overthinking, sad, but I'm sure some of you can relate.

It's like I'm the only person to go crazy while everyone else enjoys their lives well, overthinking usually has consequences in my everyday life.

Like any other addiction, any time you have a problem, you don't think you can fix it or fear that you don't have the strength to overcome it. But is your relationship irresistible enough to kill? The experience says yes. The experience says yes.

To overthink is a barricade between problem and solution–it disguises your fear of failure and makes you very cautious, depressingly motionless and even more anxious.

Most notably, it's blocking you. You lose your self-confidence and esteem in your partner. All that works in partnerships is no longer. The future is no longer about nourishing love and respect; it is nothing but a prediction of loss for an over-thinking person.

Low Self-Esteem – Root of Overthinking

You definitely know what lies underneath your intense meditations, although it may not be the easiest thing to admit. The compulsive thought goes hand in hand with rattled self-confidence and happens when you feel inadequate. In case you want to learn how to stop thinking, self-analysis may be a good way to begin.

I was tricked once and it was sufficient to make a large hole in my trust, my insecurity grew and my confidence was no longer there.

When I looked back, I felt bad for my boyfriend, if he came home late or if he didn't call when he should, my mind was going out like an alarm clock and the thoughts started to shed and I fell back into the darkness.

It took me a year to heal and trust again when my self-esteem was taken away.

It's not easy to work on a low self-esteem, but I met my friend and now my husband who knows me as I really am.

And one thing I want you to remember is that if you lack faith in yourself due of what happened to you in the past, trust them a little. Let them place you in front of the mirror and tell you how good you are, both inside and outside.

WAYS TO STOP RELATIONSHIP OVERTHINKING?

I'm not here to tell you that there's a magic to stop all these things now and forever, but I am here to share my personal tips on how to stop thinking in a relation.

Let us therefore be frank with you and move in the right direction with these suggestions below.

1. *Iron Things Out With Your Partner*

So, here's your first task: suggest a tête-au-tête as early as today. Talk Things Out with your partner Overthinking has made you a prisoner of mind, and it is essential for your thoughts to be expressed. Even if you two went through it before, now isn't the time to stop talking about things.

You know the processes of your partner by heart, so tailor what you have to say to how they respond. If you have been accused of exaggerating the problem in the past, be cool and constructive and ask them to do a little investigation. Understanding how addictive behavior functions will allow them to better understand you.

If it becomes painful and comes to a close, so be it. For a healthy relationship, you should never lack the ability to communicate your thoughts and emotions. As we know that, silence is a lack of motion, but relationships must develop and change to survive.

Stay composed, be as descriptive as you can and insist on expressing yourself. Your partner may feel confused and frightened, so be patient. Being in love means you are together in this: don't stop talking before you're also on the same page.

2. *Stop You Yourself The Moment You Find That You're Over-Analyzing The Actions Of Your Partner*

A supportive partner is a sorely needed friend to fight negative thoughts but only as long as you meet them halfway. Now that you have realized that your concerns were and remain unproductive, don't make it too complicated. Stressing how you deal with it will immediately drag you into it.

Rather, stop as soon as you catch your mind and rile up. Whether you are used to overanalyzing the expressions of your friends, dwelling on their Freudian mistakes, or obsessing about a scent of a stranger that you constantly detect on it, note that your assumptions were wrong and your thought was excessive.

3. *Make Action On Your Insecurities (It's What Makes You An Over-thinker In First Place)*

Improving your confidence is another subject, some of the things you can do as a point of departure. Silence your internal critic by acknowledging that no one is fine, and you are neither. Count every small victory, and show that you have earned the reward on your own. You can certainly appreciate it a lot–if it helps, write it down.

Be constructive, then! When you found that you overthought the actions of your partner because you were unsure of your looks, hit the gym! Perhaps your own anger or insecurity is why you stress "how they say it;" learn how to shake it out. It takes some exercise, but you can nip your overthinking in the bud as long as you take action and be positive.

4.   *Always Have Some "Me Time" Everyday*

You'll likely want to avoid those long, silent moments when all the noise in your head is overwhelming. This is not, though, when you should race alone. Have a "me" time every day, unplug the brain from the Television and telephone and come into positive thinking.

You cannot fully tone down and rest your mind until you are left alone. Nonetheless, don't allow this overthink to stop all of it. Since the lack of any diversion can cause your addictive behavior to intensify, your "me" time is great for regulation.

Try to rationalize, therefore. Don't overthink it, but deduce, if your partner does not respond to your calls. If everything's good, but you keep looking for at least one small thing to create a problem, just breathe deeply, close your eyes, and let meditation clear your brain.

5. Hang Out With Friends Who're Not Over-Thinkers

This is very important to talk to people who don't make things worse. Your logical friends probably are the last to tell you how to stop thinking in a relationship, but they can't help yet. In reality, their clear thinking is just what you need to resolve all those uncertainties.

We can and should become your everyday part of reality because they are so clear-sighted. The earlier you let your worries go, the more confusing your feelings are that nobody can understand you, the better you can resolve them and see what your problems really are.

Don't discard the views of your friends, no matter how harsh or simplified they may appear. Rational people have a completely different world view and the truth is always somewhere between them. Always be attentive to listen to what they have to say: their views that prove to be so much needed in time.

6. *Ninety Percent Of What You Stress About Won't Happen, Always Enjoy Every Good Time*

We already discussed how overthinking in a relationship almost always leads to lack of spontaneity. Perhaps it happened to you before–you want to relax and enjoy the moment, but your own feelings are all that you can think about. Awful, okay?

The fact is that most of the things you think about at that time are only fragments of your ruminant imagination. Around 90% of your worries will not be up to date, but your relationship will constantly be destroyed. Instead of thinking about how to stop in a relationship, try to be attentive and present at the moment.

And this is why it is so incredibly important to regain control of your mind. Love is not only about making plans and solving problems; it's more about building trust and allowing emotions to flood your thoughts than anything else. Do not allow those intimate moments to pass through you, but enjoy each second.

7. *Keep Your Mind Busy With What Makes You A Great Person*

Depression is similar to overthinking in some respects. If you examine your patterns more closely, you realize that over-analysis is nothing but a time delay mechanism: the longer you think of the problem, the more you actually postpone to act upon it.

What this mechanism prevents you from seeing is that it won't be resolved if the problem does exist. Why not skip ruminations and act directly? However it turns out that it will hurt less than spending hours endlessly acting out various scenarios.

Keep your mind busy with ideas instead. Work all the time on yourself and do things that will help you to become the person you want to be. Facing your challenges, you are less afraid of your constraints. Begin to work out, learn more and think less about it.

8. *Traveling with your partner at Least Once a Year*

Research shows that holiday enhances ties and helps partners to look at each other in another way. It is entirely important since these fast-paced modern times suggest a speed that not all couples can bear. Holidays are a brilliant way to escape everything and finally find time to rekindle romance.

At least once a year, travel together! When you encounter the world hand in hand, you can not only have a good time alone, but also change your minds, reflecting on what is really important. Traveling changes teaches patience and introduces serenity simply by showing you that there is a large world out there that is perhaps not so big in your everyday struggle.

9. *Ask Your Partner What Kind Of Self-Improvement Can You Do To Preserve The Relationship*

Your last task is simple: understand that you sometimes have to ask for everything you need to do. Your low self-confidence made you doubt again the actions of your partner? Tell them what's happening! In case you have a good and stable relationship, their answer will be frank and helpful.

After all, there may be some things that bother you. Yet, you should never change who you are, it does take some compromise to be in a relationship. Talk to your partner about your reservations and see if you can resolve them and how.

And don't be overly sensitive! It is very important to give your partner the opportunity to speak, even though what they have to say is not so enjoyable for you to hear. They mean well, undoubtedly, so listen to them. It's much better than trying to sort out all the feelings yourself.

10. Be with That Person That Makes You Happy

Finally, keep in mind that symbiotic relationships are not very good. Who can make you happy? A strong couple are a partnership of two strong individuals, and if you're not a solid person you can't be a strong partner first. Never stop your personal growth–it can only be counterproductive for someone you love.

If you continue to think about your partner's unhappiness or not and why it usually means that you are not happy with yourself first and foremost.

Remember that you are that independent person who has it to improve and create, which definitely is what your partner loves you so much.

Make Yourself Available And Stop Wandering

Relationships are challenging! We should be like that, so let nobody tell you otherwise. Give storytellers unconditional love and agree the true relationship requires understanding, trust and respect. If you don't know how to stop your relationship overthinking, just ask your partner.

Above all, don't get wrapped in your head-express your feelings, express your views, articulate your fears and share your doubts. Thinking over builds a wall of unproductive emotions, while thinking about them is the simplest solution. Stay strong, but articulate for your partner.

CHAPTER 11:

HOW TO RESOLVE CONFICT AND SAVE YOUR RELATIONSHIP

You are sitting in a cafeteria. Two couples sit near you in the store.

The couple on the left argue if they want to go with friends for dinner. She says, "It's never fun–the last time you said so to myself." She answers: "Of course you'd like to say that because they're my friends and you've never offered another friend a chance." War and peace, our personal edition, whatever number. "They turn away and sit in silence.

The couple on the right often explore whether they want to go with friends to have dinner. He says, "I think I'm a bit worried it'll go on for hours and it couldn't be that interesting. What do you think? What do you think?"She replies," Hey, even I know that happens. You know Jim. You know Jim. The only person who likes to talk more than him is... oh wait! That's me!

That's me!"He smiles and says,' Yeah, but I like listening to you speak. Tom, not so much. Not so much. To him, I get a bit bored–not you. She says, "I get that, I get that. I want to go, but perhaps we can arrange a time when we must leave as a compromise?"Apart from that, it will be good to get home early enough to have a great time to enjoy the rest of our night together." He smiles and nods and they keep on reading and enjoying their coffee.

Both couples had a conflict–in fact, the same one. One responded by using bad habits and used the struggle to widen a distance between them. The other used conflict as an incentive for their relationship to expand and develop. That couple think you have the best and most successful relationship? What partnership will last longer, do you think? You should look at how you and your partner handle conflicts if you are looking to understand how to save your relationship from breaking up.

Conflict Can Be Destructive

Conflict with your spouse can make you feel attacked or threatened, vulnerable and weak and so cause you back and back. When you believe that your partner is upset, you are less likely to react constructively and more likely to turn to old staff like "silent therapy," which actually is harmful than healthy. This will eventually break down the friendship.

If someone asked you if you understood how to resolve the conflict, you would probably say yes. If they asked you when quiet treatment was an appropriate way to deal with the conflict, you would nearly say no. Then, you know better than to resort to these dumb tactics, but you do so anyway if you are wounded enough. Why? Why? Why reject negative patterns instead of working to fix the communication problems?

How Conflict Can Emerge

Break the pattern of aggression and give positive energy to conflict. Don't get defensive, don't hammer the case, and don't try winning. Why would you like to lose your friend, the one you love?

Conflicts provide you and your partners with opportunities to align values and results. We are chances of knowing, appreciating and embracing disparities.

Place yourself in the role of your partner and try to understand his perspective. Such interactions and feelings may be painful, but we can never develop if we always choose comfort.

A great tactic is to use humor to break the pattern if you find yourself in a retaliatory spiral. Attempt to compete with Christopher Walken or William Shatner. Make the conflict funny.

Let's go back to the coffee shop to illustrate this point. You're seeing an elderly couple. The man spills his tea across the table by mistake and splashes and drips onto his wife's favorite outfit. He's got some napkins out, and she's laughing and joking aloud to other customers, "He's doing this to me for 20 years— never finished a cup before!"He returns, dabs her tea and jokes back to the other bosses," she asked! "She asked for it!"They both laugh, you and everybody else in the shop do too. Many people would have converted the situation into fights, but with laughter this husband and wife took the moment to nip the retaliatory spiral in his bud and turned it into an opportunity for them to laugh, enjoy and escape the argument.

Humor is a solution to solving problems in relationships. It can relieve stress and allow you and your partner to concentrate instead of what you both want.

What do you want? What do you want? What are you supposed to focus on? Remember to add, not to subtract. Every one of our partners does stuff, or has habits, which bothers us. Alternatively, concentrate on what you bring to the table, how you feel and what you enjoy. You'll find that even those things that drive you crazy are soon going to miss because they're part of the whole person, your partner, whom you love.

Use conflict as a means of aligning your values and objectives, and of injecting passion and energy into your relationship. Remember the two coffee couples? The productive couple who put their energies in knowing the needs of each other reaffirmed their love for each other— supported the need to leave at a certain time and supported their need to socialize with friends. They also played it as a compromise and promised to go home early enough to spend time together in quality.

Listen to your partner, understand what they say and why they feel like they are doing. Be truthful with your own emotions and feelings. Be your true self, as conflict is a real opportunity to connect with your partner.

Conflict is also an opportunity to find out more and love your partner even deeper. This is a chance to add spark and take your relationship to the next level. Prepare to see disagreements rather than as excuses to withdraw as changes to something better. The next time you disagree with your partner and discuss how to save your relationship, choose to see the world favorably in the case instead of the negative and take an active decision to work together toward a more stable future.

How to Create New Habits

You must be constructive to make it happen, particularly if you have to overcome your hurt feelings to figure out how to correct your relationship. You may have an exceptional store of information, skills and resources, but the point is moot if you do not have the desire to use them.

We appear to retaliate and to react with more animosity to aggression, which produces a vicious cycle that amplifies and increases a conflict's negativity. This is called the cycle of revenge and can lead to a friendship and ultimately a end. You have negative self-sabotage patterns.

What causes this? What causes this? When you focus on protecting yourself from attack rather than solving the problem that would help the relationship solve the challenge, a dispute becomes negative. By focusing on your suffering and pain, you are making sure that you experience more of the same, as you do not put your energy into one that avoids suffering and pain: looking for solutions to help you learn how to save your relationship.

Years ago, Tony Robbins took a isolated two-lane highway lined only at intervals of 10 to 20 yards with power lines. One seemed perpetually decorated in a particular snake-like area of the road with flowers, candles and photographs memorializing and honoring the life of the victims of the road that struck the post. Then, with so much space on either side of the post, how many people were killed or wounded hit it was incredible. Why was it not evaded by the victim? Why have they not swerved to either side?

It's because people's attention would be on not touching the stick. However, our focus is our direction. In case we don't want to hit the pole, we must concentrate on what we want: steer the car to each side of the pole. We can change the result by shifting our emphasis. Your relationship is the lesson. You will find yourself where you don't want your relationship to end, to struggle or get upset. Either in a miserable, unfulfilling relationship or split from your partner, you will find yourself where you don't want to be. When you concentrate on conflict resolution and evolving together, you will focus on the goals you want and achieve them. And intend to connect well with your friend. Both of you are satisfied and happy, and have the tools to build a beautiful, passionate and lasting relationship. Where emphasis flows, flows of energy.

You can turn a disagreement from something wrong into an opportunity to take your relationship to the next level by shifting your viewpoints and emphasis. It includes focus, which you are now advancing and practicing. You learn not to respond with aggression, but with positive measures to improve the relationship.

Turning Conflict into Something Positive

Break the pattern and give positive energy to conflict. Don't get defensive, pound the case, don't try to win. Don't try to win. Why would you like to lose your friend, the one you love? If you accept that there are no losers in love and you want to win together, you can focus on letting go of small arguments and on good communication.

Conflicts offer you and your partners the opportunity to align values and results. We are chances of knowing, appreciating and embracing disparities. Sit in and try to understand your partner's experience; this is how you learn to maintain a relationship. Such interactions and feelings can be painful, but we can never develop if we always opt for comfort.

Use Your Humor to Diffuse The Situation

When you find yourself in a retaliatory loop, a good tactic is to use humor to break the pattern. Take a moment to pause if you sense an argument escalating. Try to argue like Christopher Walken or Shatner. Sing a song that laughs your partner. Render the dispute amusing.

So, let us now go back to the case of the cafeteria to explain this. You're seeing an elderly couple. Accidentally, the man throws his tea around the table and splashes on the favorite dress of his friend. He's gotten ready for some treats and laughs and jokes aloud to other customers, "I've been doing it for twenty years—he's never done a cup yet!"He comes back, takes her tea off and laughs to the other managers," she asked for it!"We both chuckle, and together with everybody else in the shop you do too. Many people would have turned the situation into an argument, but with humor, this husband and wife took the moment to nip the retaliatory spiral in the bud and convert it into an opportunity to joke and to enjoy.

Humor is a Stepping Stone to Solving Relationship Issues

It can alleviate stress and allow you and your partner to concentrate on what you and your partner both want—a caring, happy relationship–rather than what you want, a needless dispute.

Once you know how to repair your relationship, you need to ask yourself some questions: What do you want? What are you supposed to focus on? Try to admire, not to weaken. Even our friends do stuff or have habits that bother us, because there is no perfect human being. Instead of focusing on your bad habits or negative behaviors, concentrate on what they bring to the table, how they make you feel and what you enjoy. You realize that you're soon going to miss even the things that made you nuts because they belong to the whole person you love, your friend.

Be the Best You Can be For Your Partner

Are you the best for your partner? Are you wondering, "How can I save my relationship? How can I save my relationship?" Use conflict as an opportunity to align your beliefs and priorities, and to instill in your relationship passion and energy. Remember the two coffee couples? The positive couple, who put energy into recognizing the need of each other, expressed their support–supported their need to leave within an hour and supported their need to speak to friends. They communicated with each other, they evaluated each other's needs and made it fun to resolve rather than allow anything small to become a major argument. They even approached it as a compromise and promised to return home early enough to have a good time together.

Listen, understand what your partner is saying, and why they feel the way they do. Be honest with your own emotions and feelings. Be your authentic self, as conflict should not be seen as the end of a relationship otherwise great; see conflict as a way to really connect with your partner.

Instead of seeing conflict as a challenge to your partner's relationship, see it as a positive tool. Conflict is also an avenue to learn more about and appreciate your partner ever more. It's a chance to add passion and bring your relationship to the next level. Learn to consider conflicts rather than as reasons for retreating as transitions to something better. When you next disagree and ask how to save your relationship, choose to see the positive rather than the negative and consciously decide to work together for a more stable future.

ESSENTIAL TIPS FOR SOLVING RELATIONSHIP CONFLICS

As everyone who has been in a romantic relationship knows, disagreements and struggles are inevitable. If two people spend a lot of time together, entangled with their lives, they are expected to disagree sometimes. Such differences can be large or small, from what to eat for dinner to whether the pair should move to a job or focus on childhood religious upbringing.

The mere fact that you clash with your partner is not an indication that your relationship is really troubled. In reality, fighting will strengthen your relationship when handled properly. You'll never fix them if you never fight and never think about your problems. You can better understand your partner and arrive at a solution that works for both of you by dealing with conflicts constructively. On the other hand, disputes can also intensify and generate ill will without anything being resolved. How can you improve the chances of effective conflict resolution in your relationship? Here are 10 tips supported by research:

1. Be direct

Often people don't just go out and clearly tell what disturbs them, but instead choose more subtle ways to express disgust. One person may talk to the other in a way that's condescensive and suggests underlying animosity. Sometimes, partners will mope and pout without really solving a problem. Partners can also simply avoid solving a question by moving subjects quickly when this issue arises or by ignoring it. These indirect ways of communicating wrath are not helpful, as they do not give a clear indication of how to respond to the person who is the object of behaviour. They know that their partner is upset, but they do not have any instructions on what they can do to resolve the problem.

2. Talk about how you feel without your partner being blamed

Statements which directly attack the character of your partner can harm the relationship especially well. If a man upset with the envy of his partner says, "You're totally irrational." A more proactive approach is to use' I declaration' and pair it with' compliance descriptions.' I statements concentrate on how you feel without criticizing your partner and comportment descriptions focus on a particular behavior that your partner does not have a character defect. For instance, this man might say,' I'm irritated, when you say that during an innocent conversation I flirt with someone.' These are direct tactics, but they do not challenge the character of your partner.

It should be noted, however, that in some situations these direct negative tactics can be constructive. Research showed that blaming and denying a partner during a conflict discussion was associated with less satisfaction in relationship over time and tended to make problems worse for couples with relatively minor problems. A different picture emerged for couples with major problems: blame and rejection attitudes directly after the dispute resolution contributed to less satisfaction, but the problems changed over the long term and this resulted in an increase in relationship satisfaction.

3. *Never say never*

You should avoid generalizing your partner when dealing with a problem. Statements such as "you never help yourself," or "you always look at your mobile phone" will probably make you defensive. Instead of encouraging a dialogue on how your partner can be more helpful or more cautious, this approach would probably lead your partner to produce counter-examples of all occasions when they were actually helpful or careful. Also, you don't want your defensive partner.

4.   *Choose your fights*

You have to stick to one issue at a time if you want a constructive debate. Unhappy pairs can pull several subjects into one discussion, a well-known conflict researcher, John Gottman, calls it "kitchen sinking." It refers to the old term" all but the sink "which means that everything was integrated. If you want to solve your own personal problems, this is probably not your strategy. Imagine thinking about incorporating more physical exercise into your daily routine. You certainly wouldn't decide this would be a perfect time to think about saving more money for retirement, organizing your wardrobe and figuring out how to manage an uncomfortable situation at work. You'd try to solve these problems one by one. This seems to be simple, but the battle over one theme can turn into a yelling session in the heat of the argument, when both partners exchange gripes. The more complaints you raise, the less likely it is that anyone will be discussed and resolved in full.

5. *Listen to your partner*

It can be somewhat frustrating to feel that you don't pay attention to your partner. When you interrupt your friend or presume you know what they think, you don't give them an opportunity to express themselves. You can still feel like you are not listening, even if you are sure where your partner is from, or know what he'll say. You can prove that you're paying attention through active listening techniques. As your partner talks, paraphrase what he's saying–that's your own words. This can prevent misconceptions before they begin. You can also test your interpretation by ensuring that you correctly interpret the reactions of your partner. For example, "You seem annoyed by that — am I correct?" Such techniques avoid confusion and show your partner that you pay attention and care about what they say.

6. *Don't automatically object to complaints from your partner*

It's tough not to get angry if you're attacked. But it doesn't solve problems with defensiveness. Imagine a couple arguing because their wife wants her husband to do more housework. If she suggests that he does a quick cleaning when he gets ready to leave in the morning, he says, "Yeah, that's going to be helpful, but I don't really have time in the morning." When she says that he's going to reserve for a while at the weekend, he says, "Sure, that could be a way to arrange it but normally, we have weekends and I'm working so it won't work." Another negative and protective behavior, when you respond to one of your partners ' grievances, is "cross-complaining." In answer to' You're not cleaning up enough around the house' for example with' You're a sweet freak.' However, it is imperative that you listen to your partner and respect what they mean.

7. *Take a different view*

While listening to your friend, you have to consider their point of view and try to understand where they come from. Those who can take their partner's viewpoint are less likely to become frustrated in a conflict discussion.

Other research has shown that it can be helpful to take a more objective approach. The researchers conducted a simple marital quality intervention in one study which asked participants to write about a certain disagreement they had with their partners from the point of view of a neutra- third party who wanted the best for the two partners. Couples who went on this 20-minute writing three times a year kept the marital satisfaction steady during the year, while couples who did not show decreases in satisfaction.

8.   *Don't disdain your partner*

Of all the negative things that you can do and do in a fight, the worst could be disdain. Gottman considered it to be the indicator number one of divorce. Disdainful comments are the ones that are insulting your spouse. Sarcasm and name-calling may be involved. It can also include nonverbal conduct, such as rolling or smirking of your eyes. This action is highly disrespectful, and it means the partner is disgusting.

Suppose one partner says, "I wish you took me out more," and the other partner replies,"Oh yeah, the most important thing to be seen and treated is to pay too heavy a price for small parts of food in a rip-off restaurant. Could you be more superficial?

9. *Don't become distracted by negativity*

It may be difficult not to answer the bad behavior of a partner with even worse behaviour. Nonetheless, encouraging this desire will only intensify the conflict. In case you and your partner poor reciprocity consequences, that is,' they are constantly exchanging angry insults and contemptuous remarks. So how much is pessimistic too much? Gottman found, in his study, that the magic number is a relation from five to one: people with five positive behaviors (for example, attempts at a good mood, warmth and cooperation) were significantly less likely to have split or separated from each negative behavior four years later.

10. *Know what time for a time-out is right*

When you find that you or your partner do not meet the above instructions, consider taking some time off from your claims. A short time out to take a breath is somewhat adequate to relax hot temperament. Conflict research shows that taking into account and managing your frustration are the secret to adequately coping with disputes. It can be constructive in your relationship to resolve your problems, but disputes must be properly managed or you risk exacerbating them.

CHAPTER 12:

FEAR OF ABANDONMEMNT AND HOW IT CAN BE TREATED

Fear of abandonment is the overriding fear that people will leave near you.

Everyone can develop a fear of giving up. It can be deeply rooted in your traumatic experience as a child or in adult depression.

When you fear failure, maintaining healthy relationships can be almost impossible. The paralyzing fear will bring you down to the wall to avoid being harmed. Or you may be sabotaging partnerships unintentionally.

The first step to overcoming the anxiety is to understand why you feel like that. You can address your fears on your own or through therapy. However, fear of abandonment may also be part of a personality disorder requiring treatment.

Continue to read and discuss the origins and long-term effects of the fear of abandonment.

Different Types of Fear of Abandonment

You may fear that someone you love will physically leave and not come back. Examples of abandonment fear. You might be afraid someone will give up your emotional needs. You can either maintain yourself in ties with a parent, partner or friend.

Fear of Emotional Abandonment

It may be less noticeable, but it is no less painful.

Emotional needs exist for us all. In case these conditions are not met, you may feel unrecognized, unloved and disconnected. You may feel very much alone, even if you are in a relationship with a physically present person.

If you have undergone emotional renunciation in the past, especially as a child, you may be constantly afraid that it will happen again.

Fear of Abandonment In Children

It is absolutely normal for babies and children to experience a period of separation fear.

You may scream, yell or refuse to let go if a parent or caregiver is leaving. At this stage, children have difficulty understanding when or if the person will return.

As they begin to understand that they come back, they resolve their terror. This happens to most children by their 3rd birthday.

Abandonment Anxiety In relationships

You can actual be afraid of allowing yourself to be insecure in a relationship. You may have problems of confidence and worry about your relationship too much. That can make your partner suspicious.

Over time, the anxieties will cause the other person to retreat and keep the cycle going.

Symptoms of The Fears Of Abandonment

When you fear abandonment, it is likely that you can identify some of these symptoms and signs:

- Too sensitive to criticism

- Trouble trusting in others

- Difficulty making friends unless you are sure you want them

- Take extreme measures to prevent rejections or separation

- Pattern of unhealthy relationships

- Staying in a relationship even at the point that it is not healthy for you

- Blaming yourself when things don't work

- Trouble committing into a relationship

- Working too hard to please people

- Getting attached to people quickly and moving on quickly

Causes of Abandonment

Abandonment problems in relationships may be due to having been emotionally or physically abandoned in the past.

For example:

- As an infant, a parent or caregiver may be dead or abandoned.

- Parental negligence may have been felt.
- Your colleagues might have rejected you.
- You have been through a loved one's chronic illness.
- A romantic partner may have suddenly left you or acted untruthfully.

These events can lead to a fear of abandonment.

Avoidant Personality Disorder

Avoidant personality disorder is a personality disorder which may include anxiety and a socially depressed or deficient sense of abandonment.

- Nervousness
- Poor self-esteem
- Extreme fear of negative judgment
- Disqualification in social settings
- Avoidance of group and self-imposed social isolation

Borderline Personality Disorder

The Borderline personality disorder is another personality disorder, where intense fear of rejection will play a part.

- Unstable relationships
- Distorted self-images
- Extreme impulsiveness
- Mood swings and anger
- Difficulty being alone

Many people who have limited personality disorders say they have been sexually or physically abused as children. Many grew up in the midst of violent strife or communities with the same illness.

Separation Anxiety Disorder

If a child does not resolve anxiety about separation and it interferes with daily work, separation anxiety disorder can occur.

The signs and symptoms include the following:

- Panic attacks
- Depression with thought of separation of loved ones
- Refusal to leave home without a loved one or to be alone
- Hallucinations with separation of loved ones

- Physics problems such as stomach pain or headache, when separated from loved ones,

Teens and adults that experience anxiety about separation.

Long-Term Effects of Fear of Abandonment

The long term effects of the fear of giving up may include:

- Challenging connections with friends and romantic partners
- Poor self-esteem
- Issues with self-confidence
- Mood swings
- Codependence
- Depression
- Fear of intimacy
- Panic problems

Examples of the fear of Abandonment

Here are a few examples of what the fear of giving up may look like:

Longer-term effects of fear of abandonment You may think, "No connection, no drop."

- You are obsessively worried about your perceived flaws and what others might think about you.
- You are the most pleasant people. You don't want to take any opportunity that someone doesn't like you to stay there.
- You are totally crushed when someone criticizes you a little or gets upset in any way.
- When you feel slighted, you overreact
- You feel insufficient and unattractive.
- You split with a romantic partner so that they can't break up.
- Even if the other person asks for space, you are clingy.
- You are often jealous, suspicious of your partner, or critical of him.

Fear of abandonment is not a diagnosed mental health disorder, but it can be certainly detected and discussed. Diagnosing fear of abandonment Fear of rejection may also be part of a diagnosable personality or other condition to be treated.

Recovery Problems

Once you know that you fear loss, you can do some things to start recovery.

Remove some slackness and stop the harsh judgment on yourself. Mind all the positive qualities that make you a good partner and mate.

Speak to the other person and how it came to be about the fear of abandonment. But be aware of what you deserve from others. Explain where you come from, but don't make something to fix your fear of abandonment. Don't expect more than is fair from them.

Work to maintain friendships and build a support network. Strong friendships will strengthen your sense of belonging and self-worth.

If this is not practical, consider talking to a qualified therapist. You will benefit from individual advice.

How to Assist Someone With Abandonment Problems

Some strategies for trying if someone you know has to deal with the fear of abandonment:

- Begin the conversation. Encourage them to speak, but don't press.
- Understand that fear is real for you, whether it makes sense or not.
- Make sure you're not going to abandon them.
- Ask what you can do to assist.
- Suggest treatment, but don't push it. If you want to start, offer your help in finding a professional therapist.

See your healthcare provider for guidance if you have attempted but are unable to manage your fear of self-abandonment or if you have signs of panic disorder, anxiety disorder or depression.

You should continue a full check-up with your primary care physician. You can then consult a doctor to diagnose and treat the illness.

Personality disorders can lead to depression, substance use and social isolation without treatment.

Fear of abandonment will affect your relationships negatively. But you can do things to minimize these fears.

If the fear of dropping out is part of a broader personality disorder, drugs and psychotherapy can be successfully treated.

BONUS: CHAPTER 13:
CONCEPT OF MARRIAGE?

The concept of a marriage is diverse and is based on cultural, religious and personal considerations by different entities.

A generally accepted and inclusive definition of marriage is this: formal and social and legal union between two people, who legally, economically and emotionally unite their lives. The formal marital arrangement usually means that, during their lives or until they wish to divorce, they have legal obligations to each other. Married also gives intimate affairs legitimacy within marriage. Traditionally, marriage is often regarded as a key factor in preserving morals and civilisation.

Marriage is governed by laws, regulations, traditions, convictions and attitudes that prescribe the rights and duties of spouses as well as agreements on the status of their offspring (if any). The universality of marriage within various societies and cultures is due to its many fundamental social and personal functions, such as sexual gratification and control, division of labour, economic production and consumption and satisfying personal needs for love, prestige and companionship. This is due to its many fundamental social and personal functions. The most important function of the system may be procreation, child care and education, socialization and the control of descent lines. Throughout the ages, marriages took many forms.

By the 21st century, in Western countries the nature of marriage— particularly with regard to the value of procreation and the ease of divorce — had started to change. In 2000, the Netherlands was the first country to recognize same-sex marriages; on 1 April 2001 the legislation came into force. Many other nations followed in the following years— including Canada (2005), France (2013), the United States (2015), and Germany (2017). Many nations have also expanded the rights and obligations of same-sex couples through a legal partnership or civil union, each meaning different things in different ways.

The complex the species, the longer the offspring relies on their mother for survival from birth to maturity, on the biological evolutionary scale. Human beings at the peak of the evolutionary level need to reach maturity most of all animals. It places further responsibilities on human parents to look after their children and marriage is generally seen as the structure that best suits certain parental duties and duties.

Marital Customs and Laws

In all human societies, past and present, some form of marriage has been identified. The meaning can be seen in the intricate and complicated laws and rituals around it. Even though these rules and practices are as complex and various as social and cultural human organizations, there are universals.

The key legal role of marriage is to guarantee the rights of spouses, to ensure freedoms and to establish children's ties in a society. Historically, marriage has granted the offspring legal status, which has entitled him to numerous rights, including the right to an inheritance, set by that community's customs. Marriage has defined the appropriate social relationships for the offspring in many cultures, including the suitable selection of future spouses.

Marriage was seldom a matter of free will until the late 20th century. In Western societies, marriage was linked to love between women, but even in Western cultures (as writers ' novels such as Henry James and Edith Wharton attest) romantic love did not become the prime motive of marriage for most centuries, and the marriage partner was carefully selected.

Endogamy, the oldest social rule for marriage is endogamy, the custom of marrying someone of one's own tribe or community. If the forms of communication with external groups are restricted, the inevitable consequence of endogamous marriage is. In some cultures, cultural pressures to marry within the social, economic and ethnic group tend to be strongly implemented.

Exogamy, the custom of marriage outside a group, is found in societies with the most complex relationships, thus excluding large groups which can trace their lines towards a common ancestor.

Marriages are typically regulated by the family in communities in which the large or extended family is the basic unit. It is believed that love between the spouses comes after marriage, and the social benefits that the larger family gain from the match are taken into account. By comparison, young adults typically choose their own partners in cultures where the small or nuclear family predominates. Love precedes (and determines) marriage and the socioeconomic aspects of the match are normally given less thought.

The almost common practice in businesses of arranged marriages is that anyone behaves as an agent or as an intermediary. The main responsibility of this person is to arrange a marriage suitable for the two families represented. In cultures that promote marriages, some kind of dowry or spousal property is almost always traded.

Dating is the most typical way for individuals to meet and meet prospective partners in communities in which people choose their own partners. Successful dating may lead to courtesy, usually leading to marriage.

PERSISTENT MYTHS ABOUT MARRIAGE

Some myths have been derived from pop culture. Of example, the persistent myth is that when you are with "the one," your relationship should be simple, "says Jazmin Moral LCSW-C, a psychotherapist specializing in working with couples in Rockville, Md.

Other misunderstandings may be born closer to home—within our own families. You will assume that all disputes are poor and marked by chaos if your parents can not disagree without screaming and shouting insults. You might expect to fight with your grandparents if your parents constantly argued with you and made comments criticizing all lawyers.

If your family believes strongly in what a good matrimony looks like and regularly expresses this conviction, you could have internalized it yourself.

The issue with myths is that they can actually undermine our relationships when we confuse them for reality. Below are seven common myths and their reality.

1. Myth: Your true love knows what to say and do immediately to make you happy

Fact: "There is a fear that it won't' count' or that it isn't as meaningful if you've got something to ask for," Moral said. Since our spouses are unable to read our minds, it is important to communicate our desires in a marriage for each of us.

Communication is also critical when couples have dispute or disconnection. After a misunderstanding, several partners would allow the building of their frustration while quietly hoping that their loved one will discover what they did wrong, or think it is so clear that they do not have to spell it out. Generally speaking, it is important to put your relationship first, as "it doesn't happen magically. You must make it a priority and speak to each other vulnerably, "Moral said.

2. **Myth: In marriage there is a universal path, like having children**

Fact: "There are no rules other than those which the couple honestly and openly agree with," said Monica O'Neal of Harvard, PsyD, a licensed Harvard clinical psychologist, relationship specialist, author and lecturer. Before she married, she suggested couples establish their own sense of marital culture. In other words, think about how you feel about marriage.

If people try to take major lifestyle choices, such as children, follow the popular or conventional path — unless their desires and values are taken into consideration — only leads to problems.

3. **Myth: Kids put families back together**

Fact: Keith Miller, LICSW, a couple therapist in Washington DC, and the author of the forthcoming book, Love-Under-Repair: How to Save Your Marriage and Survive Couple Therapy, said that having children will improve one another's understanding and intimacy. However, having children also "activates many previously hidden spousal fault lines. Some of these fault lines lead to disastrous marital disasters that nobody seemed to be seeing. "According to Miller, for example, spouses may disagree about parental behavior. One wife may think that the other is too permissive, while the wife swears that they are too restrictive. One spouse may become jealous if the other spouse is always helped by his child. As most parents have a natural instinct to protect their children, instead, they will attack their wife, he said.

"If you allow your life to expand to take up the wisdom of' it takes a village' you will get closer to having children," Miller said. This includes learning from others and building a network that supports and encourages "the normal pressure to have a mother or dad." There are also numerous helpful parenting resources, such as the Parent Encouragement Program (PEP).

4.   Myth: Differences are going to ruin your marriage

Fact: It is not the marriage differences that could kill them, Miller said. That's how we react to these differences, he said. "We fall in love with our partner... We diminish our differences and forget that we are two people who are completely separate." But after the lunar phase is over we remember that we are indeed two different people, and we freak out of them. But, it is very crucial to realize that there are natural and normal variations. You don't have to comply with all your partner does, said Miller. "From where they're coming from you could find something worthwhile." If you can't, he said, get curious. You might say, for example, "I don't get this. Would you help me to understand that? Can you bring me where you are? "We give couples the chance to connect and get to know each other," he said. Once we fall in love, he said, we still share our stories. Try to do the same after you're married. Because once you can put your ideas to one side for the time being, to listen fully to your spouse, you'll find something you can say in the details of her story.

5. Myth: Cheerful couples argue not

Fact: Morally, each of us gets married with different expectations, desires, concerns and experiences of our families or past relationships. "Miscommunication is bound to happen, of course." Actually, O'Nealsaid, "a lack of argument shows a lack of truth and emotional intimacy." When couples argue not, all manner of emotional compromises occur, from communicating to approaching time with the extended family, she said.

This also erodes faith and induces feelings of disgust, she said. Everyone in the relationship–including the children–will experience an uncomfortable stress or a feeling of' walking on eggshells' inside the home, but will not be able to talk about it or hesitate to embrace it.' It makes marriage and household "tenuous and dysfunctional." Nonetheless, they "do not fire, strike below the belt or use the point as a means of gaining power in the relationship," said O'Neal. "The healthiest couples always try to resolve conflicts, can respond to the agreements and then forgive and move on."

6. Myth: Happy couples must do all together

Fact: It is great to spend time together and to share common interests, but it is healthy to focus on your own interests, said Moral. In fact, if something is the opposite— you are forced to do things that you do not like or you can't do things important to you— your sense of security and confidence in your marriage is jeopardized, she said.

It may lead to resentment or feeling trapped by marriage if we don't feel supported in pursuing our interests or goals."

7. *Myth: Monogamy means love and dull sex to dissipate*

Fact: "In an enduring relationship the sexual excitement does not take over when you first meet a person, but it's a deeper excitement that develops by learning to know someone intimately and deeply." When couples buy into the myth of the fading passion, they can resign themselves to an unsatisfactory sexual life rather than work together to resolve the problem.

"The aim is to emotionally connect and develop a stable relationship with your partner. Emotional transparency and love expressiveness go hand in hand with physical pleasure in bed. "Marriage is not" something that will hold itself together, "said Miller. It is important to work constantly on your relationship, don't take yourself for granted and take conscious choices to be caring and loving.

A GOOD MARRIAGE IS A HAPPY MARRIAGE

A healthy marriage makes both partners feel safe. Only when there is a basis for protection will individuals and the couple grow and mature. Intimacy is possible only if people feel safe enough to be vulnerable. Any conflict without it threatens the whole relationship.

It is possible that some of the people I see in counseling will end their marriages. Some certainly should never have happened at all. These are the couples who were unable to establish and maintain their partnership with others. Some of them married for all the wrong reasons: to get out of a parent's house for money, or just because everyone else expected them. Many combat verbal, physical or emotional violence. In-such situations, it is important to ensure the protection of individuals first. Only then should a couple think about trying again.

Nonetheless, most of the couples I saw in practice do not battle the repercussions of marriage without love or violence. They have come for advice because they long for the link they once had or they don't function. "We can't communicate" means "we're not communicating," and it often does not feel sufficiently comfortable for one or both of them to be 100% connected.

Loving alone isn't adequate. Security depends on attitudes and behaviours, which foster emotional connection and deep mutual respect. If one felt insecure, distrustful or challenged emotionally, marriage would obviously not work in the long-term. It may last — for many reasons, people remain in unsatisfactory relationships. But it's not going to be personal.

A marriage-should be a safe place for every partner to be loved, respected and seen and to have a strong sense of cohesion. A good marriage is one where each partner works regularly on the following security elements:

- ***Security***

Safety depends on ensuring that the other person is committed to the promise of commitment and does everything he can to fulfill this promise. Every wedding has rough patches. Each marriage has periods when the partners feel out of sync. Commitment to commitment ensures that the issues are dealt with by both parties.

They're not disengaging or bailing. We don't allow themselves to lay blame. Each of them has a duty and works hard to fix their role in the that gap between them.

- ***Trust***

Confidence is a gift that we give to someone we love. It's a fact in a healthy marriage. Everybody knows that the other person would never do anything to break their hearts. You treat it as the precious commodity because you realize that once destroyed, it is very difficult to recover trust. Couples who are last couples who do not betray the faith. Since trust is so important for security and because circumstances can be misread neither leaps to conclusions about treason. Instead, they speak through one of the partners when they feel betrayed.

- ***Honesty***

All partners must be frank with each other in order to trust. Since neither of them has anything to hide, phone and computer passwords are exchanged. Their investments, actions and relationships are real. You understand that a couple are a team of two and each of them needs the integrity of the other to function.

- *Mutual respect*

In healthy marriages, the partners appreciate and love the other person, and often say so. We respect the opinions, goals, thoughts and feelings of each other. You listen carefully and are ready to learn from each other. Neither speak to the other nor make disdainful expressions or commentaries that invalidate the other's ideas or feelings.

- *Fidelity*

Fidelity means various things to various people. It is not beneficial to say that when you think about it, you both of course have the same thing in mind. A happy couple have spoken openly and honestly about how they interpret "cheating" and their expectations of each other. You make a mutual agreement that you intend to uphold.

- *Platinum Rule*

It is a good rule, but the Platinum rule takes things a step further: "Treat someone as they want to be handled." It means taking the time to consider and to do what most respects and pleases your partner even if you don't want that to be.

- ***Emotional accessibility***

The partners are emotionally involved in successful marriages. All frequently show love. They both share their thoughts and emotions and are open to their mate. If conflict occurs, no one shuts down mentally. Alternatively, they meet and support each other while working through anything that is disturbing.

- ***Clean fighting***

Sure. Yes. Sometimes everyone loses it. But one can be upset without the other individual being weakened. Calling, bullying, intimidating, threatening to leave or throw out the other person are aspects of dirty struggles. Those who deal with a dispute by physical or emotional violence never settle it. Usually, the situation is much worse than it had to be.

Sanitary couples know how to fight with dignity. I don't blame them. Rather, they speak from their own feelings and experiences.

Last marriages are founded on health. Without the relationship, no member of the couple will relax. Every person thereby becomes a better version of themselves and marriage becomes stronger and more intimate.

CONCLUSION

Anxiety can be an assassin of ties. Even if a relationship remains unchanged in the face of such fears, it will never develop fully. Whether your wife, children, friends or siblings are involved, anxiety is your enemy.

Don't give in. Don't have such doubts to live comfortably. Instead, find out how you unintentionally accommodated this fear and then do the opposite. Give yourself corrective interactions that reverse fear and give you the freedom to maximize each relationship.

One place to start is to use the details we have just discussed. Or you can think about joining a support group if you're in the Folsom area. Therapy can also be very effective. My colleagues and I would be happy to help but if you are searching for other sources of support in or around Folsom California, it can be that it might be of benefit to the Valley Psychological Center or the Place Within.

If you battle anxiety about relationships, don't delay tackling the problem. When you start making improvements, you will find that it is easier to solve, and life is far more complete than you could have expected.